THE DERRYDALE PRESS
FOXHUNTERS' LIBRARY

FOXHUNTING
WITH
MELVIN POE

Peter Winants

For my old friend
J. B. Secor
Peter Winants

Published in association with
The National Sporting Library

THE DERRYDALE PRESS
Lanham and New York

THE DERRYDALE PRESS

Published in the United States of America
by The Derrydale Press
4720 Boston Way, Lanham, Maryland 20706

Distributed by NATIONAL BOOK NETWORK, INC.

Copyright © 2002 BY THE DERRYDALE PRESS

Library of Congress Control Number: 2002106888
ISBN 1-58667-097-2 (cloth : alk. paper)

FOXHUNTING WITH MELVIN POE

Other books by the author:

Jay Trump, A Steeplechasing Saga
Flatterer, The Story of a Steeplechase Champion
Steeplechasing: The Complete History of the Sport in North America

---

CONTENTS

Acknowledgments

I am indebted to the following institutions and persons:

The National Sporting Library for research.

The Chronicle of the Horse magazine for providing photographs.

George L. Ohrstrom for the encouragement in making this book a reality.

The Poes for giving hundreds of hours for interviews, and others who provided their thoughts on Melvin.

John and Kerry Glass for giving me access to several tapes of interviews with Melvin and Albert Poe.

Norman Fine, James L. Young, John Coles and Margaret II. Whitfield for reviewing the text.

Elizabeth R. Manierre for the sketches for the chapter heading and the map on page 23.

Mark and Joy Smith of Lost Mountain Graphics for layout and design.

The Derrydale Press for publishing short-run sporting books that otherwise would not be published.

Foreword

I can't remember when there hasn't been a Melvin. We're related in a distant way by blood and in a closer way by avocation. His influence on my life was subtle and quiet, much like Melvin, except when he's cheering hounds to a viewed fox. I have followed him on foot, by car and on a horse. I only wish I'd paid more attention.

My great uncle, Ray Pearson, lived at the Old Dominion kennels and whipped in to Melvin. I learned to crack a whip while straddling a fence outside Old Dominion's tack room. It was a magical place. Tall saddle racks stood on the floor, large enough to hold two saddles and two kids. My cousins and I held imaginary hunts and races on those horses. Whips and horns hung along the walls next to bridles with shiny silver bits. We took turns trying to blow Melvin's old cow horn to see who could get the biggest response from the hounds. When Melvin drove in, we would try to hide the whips that we had beaten the ends off in vain attempts at cracking them.

"Hellooo," Melvin would say in his high-pitched voice as he went about opening the doors and gates on the kennels. Hounds poured forth from the lodges and ran all over the barnyard. He would hop back in his truck, start down the lane and holler, "Hey, come on hyere." The scattered hounds would form a teeming mass of tongues and tails behind the pickup and disappear down the narrow road.

Melvin is the Pied Piper of houndom, and he has the same effect on people. His quick wit and full understanding of exactly who he is puts him at ease with himself and others. Nor is he easily impressed. One of the Orange County masters brought a visitor to the kennel after the Virginia Hound Show one year. They were greeted with Melvin's usual "hellooo." The visitor was introduced as Lord Something or other who hunted the Whatever. Observing that this hadn't impressed Melvin, the master added, "He's from England." "Oh," said Melvin, "that's okay, we won't hold that against him."

There was a pretty English lady, though, that did get Melvin's attention. Elizabeth Taylor, when married to John Warner, became fond of Melvin's home-brewed wine and attended Orange County's annual landowners' picnic, which was hosted by Melvin and Peggy. That gave the natives of Hume, Virginia, something to talk about.

Melvin is a man who has enjoyed his life's work, and he's made it enjoyable for countless others. He was born to what became his profession and passion. As a member of a large family, he and his brothers roamed the hills and forests surrounding their home at Hume, learning the ways of the woods and animals. Hunting for deer, turkey and other game wasn't in those days just a pastime. It helped feed the family as well as being fun.

Foxhunting was a huge part of the social happenings in this rural community, and the Sunday turnout hunts (described in Chapter 2) played an important role in Melvin's childhood. This was the cradle of the Virginia foxhound and the home of famous foxhunting families. The Chadwell, Kines, Putnam, Pearson and Bywaters families all lived nearby, and Sterling Larrabee hunted what now is the Old Dominion territory. As described in Chapter 3, Larrabee's hounds, running in full cry past the schoolhouse at Hume's crossroad, proved to be an inspiration for a young schoolboy.

Except for a stint in the army, Melvin has lived near his birthplace his entire life. His farm is a stone's throw from the baseball field where he often spent Sunday afternoons. He's a true sportsman. He's enjoyed jousting tournaments, plays a mean version of croquet, and he rarely misses steeplechase meets or games on television of his beloved Oriole and Redskin teams.

Foxhunting, though, is his first love. His childhood gave him the knowledge of the wild that he's used throughout his career. He often amazes followers with "lucky guesses" to set the pack straight after a loss. These "guesses" were from knowing the lay of the land and how a fox would traverse it, knowledge gained by countless hours in the woods and keen observation.

Melvin allows his hounds to do the hunting, helping out only when he's sure that the hounds can't solve the puzzle on their own. He slips along quietly, encouraging them with his voice and very little use of the horn. The hounds love him. He is in fact a hound magnet. While recuperating from hunting mishaps, Melvin had to refrain from following the hunt in his truck because the hounds would always find him instead of the fox.

When Melvin was asked if he likes large numbers of foxhunters in the field, he replied, "Bob Hope didn't want to play to an empty house. If you're hunting for yourself, then that's one thing, but if you're working for a club, then the more the merrier."

I recently stopped by the Poe's farm. Peggy was sitting in the yard, looking across the road at the rolling hills. "Mel's over there, alone with his hounds. They were running, but they've gone quiet now."

At eighty-one years, the joy of the chase has never diminished for Melvin, and it never will. It's a virus contracted in his youth that has glowed just below fever pitch throughout his life. Like a lot of viruses, it will infect you if you stand too close to the carrier. We should all be so lucky.

Tommy Lee Jones

WARRENTON, VIRGINIA
MARCH 2002

Tommy Lee Jones (left, the author of the foreword) hunted with Melvin Poe and the Bath County Hounds at George L. Ohrstrom's Fassifern Farm, Warm Springs, Virginia, in 2001. Tommy Lee embarked upon his

thirty-second year as huntsman of the Casanova (Va.) Hunt in the 2001-2002 season. His articles on foxhunting frequently appear in the magazine In and Around Horse Country.

Introduction

Charley Matheson, a former president of the Orange County Hunt, hit the nail on the head when talking about his friend Melvin Poe in Chapter 8. "Everybody likes to be around him," Charley said. "People are drawn to him, love to get his insight into things they're very interested in."

So true. I've seen this time and again in the ten years I've really gotten to know Melvin, when we've been hunting together with the Bath County Hounds in west central Virginia. Oh, of course, I knew him casually for quite a few years prior to that. I hunted with him a couple times at Orange County and rode against him in old-fashioned point-to-point races. I sensed he was a unique character, but it took our days at Bath County for me to truly put a handle on what makes Melvin Poe tick, and that's when I came to realize that he's better at drawing a crowd than anyone I've ever known.

When foxhunters gathered in the farmhouse at Bath County after a day's hunting, it was a cinch to spot Melvin. But, actually, it was hard to pick him out, because he was the guy everyone was crowded around. The guy everyone was drawn to. The guy they wanted to talk to, as Charley pointed out, because they'd get insight into things of mutual interest.

Then there was Virginia Hunt Week, when seven or so hunts, including Bath County, banded together to host consecutive days of foxhunting, one at each hunt. We thought we wouldn't get a big crowd because Bath County is off the beaten track, and foxhunters wouldn't hunt each day. Most would surely take a day off, and we assumed they wouldn't travel over the mountains to hunt with us. Wrong. The first year, we had a field of 79, far too many for our poor little hunting country. The attraction wasn't Bath County, per se, rather Melvin Poe, and after hunting, throngs gathered around him at the hunt breakfast.

We'll fix 'em on Hunt Week the following year, we thought, when to keep the crowd down foxhunters had the choice of two meets on the same day, at Bath County and another hunt. There was some improvement, but little Bath County far outdrew the other fixture, and you know why.

The typical visit to Bath County doesn't involve large crowds, as in Hunt Week. Usually, it's four or five invited guests from the Middleburg area, and a like number of local foxhunters. In evenings after hunting, we'd sip a little of Melvin's home-brewed wine and listen to his stories. Over the ten-year period, I've heard tons of these stories, and occasional repeats. Nor was the evening chatter limited to colorful anecdotes. Melvin also discussed the finer points of happenings in the hunting field that day, what the fox did and didn't do, when hounds best reacted to situations and conditions that either enhanced or deterred the day's sport. During these sessions I invariably thought I should have a tape recorder to create an oral history of the man whom I describe in Chapter 1 as the last of a vanishing breed. No dice. I was having too good a time and learning too much about foxhunting to worry about oral histories and such.

In the winter of 2001, however, I took my tape recorder each Wednesday afternoon in January through March to the Poe farmhouse at Hume, Virginia, and recorded his thoughts. Peggy was present, I'm glad to say, because she had valuable comments, and she whipped us back on the line when we wandered off the subject. We ended up with a mess of tapes, and the pages that follow will describe the life and foxhunting philosophy of an extremely talented and charismatic man who invariably draws a crowd.

Peter Winants

MIDDLEBURG, VIRGINIA
FEBRUARY 2002

CHAPTER 1

HAPPY BIRTHDAY, MELVIN

AUGUST 24, 2000 – BATH COUNTY HOUNDS, WARM SPRINGS, VIRGINIA

T HE SOFT voice of huntsman Melvin Poe encouraged 8½ couple of American foxhounds while drawing a dense pine covert on George Ohrstrom's Fassifern Farm. It was quiet, serene, beautiful. The tranquility, though, came to a screeching halt when strike hound Carlisle, drafted from the Orange County Hunt, feathered, then opened. Melvin's voice rose to the intensity of a rebel yell when other pack members honored Carlisle. Memories of the fun are preserved by an entry for the day's sport in my hunting diary:

> "This was the precise day of Melvin's eightieth birthday. Hounds celebrated the occasion by immediately finding a fox in the Guest House Covert, and we had a three-quarter-hour chase through Upper Fassifern and back to the Haynes farm. Scenting wasn't good, but hounds picked at the line, worked hard, and the field of eight was right in Melvin's pocket, enjoying great hound work. What fun. This is what foxhunting is all about. Happy birthday, Melvin."

Melvin and Peggy Poe celebrated Melvin's eightieth birthday in 2000.
Grandson Christopher Gould is in the foreground.

This wasn't a big deal, though, to Melvin, not that he didn't appreciate the birthday present from his hounds. At the time, he'd been a professional huntsman for more than fifty years, first with the Old Dominion Hounds and the Orange County Hunt in northern Virginia, two of America's finest hunts, then with the Bath County Hounds, a private, unrecognized hunt whose territory consists of valleys in the Allegheny Mountains of west-central Virginia, near the West Virginia line. Through the years, Melvin has provided sport for thousands of foxhunters and has become a legend in his own time. I am one of the lucky ones, having ridden behind Melvin for ten seasons as Bath County's field master.

I was a bit sad after the glow of Melvin's eightieth birthday hunt had worn off. The sport at Bath County solely revolves

Melvin Poe was raised in Hume, Virginia, where the Blue Ridge Mountains are a backdrop for gently rolling farmland in the northern corner of the territory of the Old Dominion Hounds. General Patton's Cobbler Hunt hunted the area in 1920-1942.

Melvin Poe used a cow horn when hunting the hounds for 16 seasons for the Old Dominion Hounds and in the early years of his 27-year tenure with the Orange County Hunt. He switched to the English horn after the cow horn ground into his ribs a few times during falls. The picture was taken in 1964.

Hume was the birthplace of many famous fox-hunters, including members of the Chadwell family. Elias Chadwell was the huntsman of the Millbrook Hunt in New York in 1928-1950, when succeeded by his son Earl.

around Melvin. It would be naïve to think that this fun can go on forever, and when Melvin steps down it will be the end of an era.

Melvin is a member of a dying breed. As the countryside continues to disappear in many sections of America, the likes of Melvin Poe are becoming few and far between in an urbanized society. Today, we simply don't have young men (or ladies) who, like Melvin, have inherited a love of hunting from their fathers and grandfathers; have been with hounds since day one; have studied foxes, know them personally; know every inch of the countryside, and ride well enough to cross it; know all animals and are expert woodsmen and farmers; and who dearly love what they're doing and whose enthusiasm, showmanship and charisma are contagious.

The area around Hume, Virginia, where Melvin was born and raised, was real country, truly in the boondocks in Melvin's youth. "For entertainment, the only things we had were church activities, an occasional baseball game and our hounds, and of course we had to work long and hard to make a living off the soil," Melvin said.

William (Buster) Chadwell, right in the painting by Else Tuckerman, was huntsman of the Essex Foxhounds in New Jersey in 1944-1977, when succeeded by his son Rodney (center). Buster's father, Ned, was huntsman of the Orange County Hunt in 1919-1924, then Mr. Larrabee's Hounds until 1930.

Hume, about 18 miles north and west of Warrenton, has gently rolling countryside and a combination of small coverts and large pieces of woodland. Mountains in the Blue Ridge chain with colorful names like Oven Top, Big Cobbler, Rattlesnake and Buck are in the immediate background. Today, the area around the tiny crossroad of Hume is changing due to the proximity of Interstate 66, which connects Washington, D.C., 65 miles to the east, and Interstate 81, a north-south artery to the west. This has resulted in the carving out of farmettes and the construction of ostentatious McMansions. Still, lots of lovely countryside remains, and it's hunted by the Old Dominion Hounds, while the Rappahannock Hunt has the territory to the southwest and Warrenton Hunt is to the southeast. General Patton's Cobbler Hunt had a territory south of Hume in 1920-1942.

The Poe family has been prominent in Fauquier and Rappahannock counties for generations. North Poe Road and South Poe Road, named for Melvin's great grandfather, wind through these counties today.

The Poes are one of America's best-known foxhunting families. Melvin's

Albert Poe (Melvin's brother) was the huntsman of the Piedmont Foxhounds in 1954-1974, then the Fairfax and Middleburg hunts for 19 years. The photograph is of the Piedmont pack crossing Panther Skin Creek in 1960.

brother, Albert, was huntsman for the Piedmont Fox Hounds for 20 years commencing in 1954. His breeding program resulted in a renowned pack of American foxhounds, the offspring of which are found in packs throughout the United States. Albert later carried the horn for the Fairfax and Middleburg hunts.

Equally famous are the Chadwells, also natives of Hume. Ned Chadwell was huntsman of the Orange County Hunt in 1919-1924, when he went with Mr. Larrabee's Hounds (the forerunner of the Old Dominion) until retiring in 1930. Ned's brother, Elias, was huntsman of the Millbrook (N.Y.) Hunt in 1928-1950, when succeeded by his son, Earl. Famed author Gordon Grand, a regular foxhunter with Millbrook, thinly disguised Elias as fictitious huntsman "Will Madden" in several books published by The Derrydale Press in the 1930s.

Meanwhile Ned Chadwell's son William, nicknamed "Buster," Melvin's contemporary, went to the Essex (N.J.) Fox Hounds at age 15 as second whipper-in, then on to the Fairfield and Westchester Hunt in Connecticut as first whip until departing in 1941 for army duty in World War II. Upon his discharge in 1944, Buster became Essex's huntsman, and, like Melvin, became a legend for providing sport in the field and at hound shows. Buster's son, Rodney, became Essex's first whip at age 17 in 1965, and has been huntsman upon the retirement of Buster in 1977.

Elias and Buster Chadwell, both deceased, are among the 26 huntsmen that have been honored by inclusion in the Huntsman's Room at the Museum of Hounds and Hunting, Leesburg, Virginia. Melvin Poe will surely one day achieve this ultimate honor for American huntsmen.

In addition to the Poe and Chadwell families, the Ballard, Welch, Pearson, Putnam and Kines families, all of Hume, were enthusiastic hound breeders and foxhunters. Also, Ennis Jenkins, whose son Rodney gained

fame in show jumping, kept hounds at nearby Flint Hill, and Burrell Frank Bywaters, who bred and sold hundreds of hounds to recognized hunts in the first three decades of this century, lived at Culpeper, 50 or so miles south of Hume. Burrell Frank's son, Hugh, was Warrenton's huntsman for several seasons in the 1930s; his grandson, Dick, was Warrenton's huntsman in 1938-1973. "When I was a kid, Burrell Frank Bywaters was very elderly, but I can remember him driving a buggy up from Culpeper, with his hounds trailing on behind, to hunt with my father and other friends around Hume. He hunted the hounds from his buggy," said Melvin.

CHAPTER 2

THE SPORTING HERITAGE
OF THE POE FAMILY

ELVIN'S grandfather, John Lewis Poe—born and raised near Amissville, 20 or so miles from Hume—fought for the Confederates in Civil War battles at Seven Pines, the second battle of Manassas, Harpers Ferry, Winchester, Antietam and Gettysburg.

John Lewis stated in the Poe family album that he inadvertently saved the life of his brother, Billy, at Antietam. "Billy was hit by a bullet which struck a pocket-book in his coat pocket. I had given him this pocket-book several days before to buy something to eat, and he hadn't given it back. It turned the bullet and saved his life."

Union troops captured John Lewis's unit near Cumberland, Maryland, in August 1864. "We'd had skirmishes at Hancock and Old Tavern near Cumberland. We then came down the Moorefield Valley and camped. We'd been marching day and night, and the whole crowd was broken down. Averill's Brigade came upon us that night and captured our picket. They caught us all asleep and got about 450 of us without the fire of a gun. I never hated anything so badly in my life," John Lewis said.

The captives marched for several days, then boarded a train to

Melvin Poe plays with foxhound puppies at the age of 12 in 1932.
His brother, Jim, is in the center, Jack Thompson on the left.

Wheeling, West Virginia, and on to Camp Chase near Columbus, Ohio. "We stayed there for about eight months," John Lewis wrote. "I didn't know what it was to get enough to eat but twice while I was there. Three crackers and a piece of pickle pork was a day's rations."

John Lewis departed Camp Chase for Richmond in March 1865 for prisoners' exchange. "Marco Davis [a friend] and I walked all the way from Richmond to Amissville [approximately 125 miles]. It took us five days."

Following the war, John Lewis married the former Agnes Dulaney Anderson, and struck out on his own to lease the Norton farm at the base of Big Cobbler Mountain near Hume. There, he raised five

Ollie Poe, who died in 1966 at the age of 80, was the father of Melvin and Albert and eight other children.

children, one being Ollie, who was Melvin's father. In 1914, Ollie married Eva Pearson, a member of a family that is as well known as the Poes in the area.

Eva and Ollie bought a farm on the Rappahannock River, 3½ miles west of Hume, and proceeded to raise ten children, a like number of boys and girls. "We were in a kind of rotation—a boy, then a girl, then two boys and two girls—right down the line," said Melvin, who was the third child. Albert, eleven years younger than Melvin, was the eighth. Five of the children were living as of 2001.

School Days

Ollie Poe's children went to public school at Hume. "No buses in those days," said Melvin. "We rode ponies to school, or, sometimes, three on a horse, or at other times in a buggy. Made no difference, we got there one way or another, and we'd often have races to see who'd get home first." At school, the ponies were kept in a barn on the school grounds. The principal and one

The family farmhouse at Hume was the birthplace of the 10 Poe children.

of the teachers arrived in buggies. Their horses remained hitched in run-in stalls during school hours.

Melvin fondly remembers annual Easter egg hunts at school. "Each of us brought a couple eggs, which teachers hid around the school yard, and each class had a turn," Melvin said. "Being a real country boy, I knew where to look, and I'd find the most eggs. One year, I had thirteen eggs and was proud as punch. I ate a couple and put the rest in my pockets. That day, I walked home, but Uncle Pete [Pearson] rode by and said, 'Hop on, I'll give you a lift.' Somehow, when cantering, I managed to dig my feet into the horse's flank, and he went to bucking. Off I went and busted all my eggs. It was a sad day."

Melvin also remembered rabbit hunts during recesses at school. "One winter's day there was a light snow, and we saw tracks. We tracked up—ran after them, no traps or anything, we were fast little country boys—and caught six or eight rabbits at recess, and put 'em in a box to keep at the schoolhouse overnight. We came in the next morning to find an empty box, no rabbits. It seems the principal had turned them loose. We weren't pleased, but we went tracking again that recess, most likely caught the same rabbits."

The students occasionally encountered foxhunters at the crossroad in

Melvin inspects the swimming hole at the camp for Boy Scouts at the Poe farm on the Rappahannock River. Ollie Poe and his sons built the bunkhouse in the background.

Hume. "One morning, there was a meet there of the Cobbler Hunt. The principal—all of us—got tied up by the hunters on the way to school. No problem, school started an hour late that morning."

Melvin also recalled a day when Old Dominion's foxhounds ran a deer (carted deer hunts are described in chapter 3) through the village. "I was in class and looked out the window and saw horses with people in red coats galloping down the road, followed by a loose horse flying along behind. I told my teacher that a neighbor owned the horse, and he must have jumped out. I asked to be excused to help catch him. Well, I didn't worry about the horse, but ran down to an abandoned cabin, where the hounds bayed the deer. In time, a cart pulled by mules—the fastest trotting mules I ever seen—came to pick up the deer and return her to the kennels. By then, school was out and I rode my pony home, but the excitement stayed on for a long time."

Melvin became a Boy Scout as a teenager. "I was nicknamed 'Nature Boy' because everyone turned to me when they wanted to find out something about nature—identifying trees, birds and tracks of animals, things like this, which I knew more about than the Scoutmaster," said Melvin. When

The Poe farm is now the property of Lynn R. Coleman. Old Dominion's pack of fox-hounds frequently hunts the area, which is paneled with coops and log fences.

school buses came into use, there was no need for the barn at the school. Ollie and his children tore it down and used the lumber to build a Scout camp on their farm alongside the Rappahannock River. The campsite was named "Seven Gates" because of the number of gates encountered between the county road and the camp.

In time, Melvin became the assistant Scoutmaster. "A lot I learned in the Scouts helped me in the army and all through life," he said. Though the ownership of the Poe farm has changed hands through the years, various Scout troops continue to use the campgrounds, and the structure built with lumber from the school's barn is still in use.

Being considerably younger, Albert had the luxury of school buses. "The bus picked me up on a macadam road a bit over half a mile from the farmhouse," Albert said. "I remember several mornings when we'd had a lot of rain and the dirt road was a mess. I talked Melvin into carrying me piggyback to the bus." Melvin said it wasn't a big deal to carry Albert. "He was little and light."

Hounds and Hunting

Ollie Poe kept six to eight hounds, some with Bywaters bloodlines. Also, Ollie was friendly with Old Dominion's huntsman, Will Putnam, who sometimes gave him hounds that were too shy, or because of cutbacks due to the approach of World War II. Ollie's hounds were versatile. "When we got on horses, they knew it was to hunt fox," Melvin said. "On foot when we had rifles, they knew to hunt rabbits. When we picked up a lantern at night, they'd automatically hunt skunks, possums and raccoons. We didn't think there was anything unusual about this, that everyone's hounds were like this."

Melvin said that skunk hides sold for $2.50, and the same with raccoons and possums, while fox hides were more valuable, at $4.50 or $5.00. The sale of hides supplemented the 50 cents a day that Ollie paid his children for working on the family farm. "We'd never kill a fox. He was our sporting animal," Melvin said.

The Poe children hunted the ponies that they rode to school. A Dr. Elliott of Markham bred these ponies and farmed them out to children in the area to be ridden and schooled, then took them back to be sold as made ponies. Melvin clearly remembers the first time he jumped a chicken coop on one of Elliott's ponies. "I was about eight years old and riding with Uncle Walter. He jumped a coop on his big old horse and called back to me, 'Come on, your pony can do it.' We flew over, and then there was no stopping me."

All of Ollie's neighbors had riding horses or workhorses. "When I was young, there was no such thing as a pick-up truck or tractor on our farm, horses did it all," Melvin said. He said his mother didn't ride, but she hitched a horse to a buggy to go to the store and to church activities. Eva Poe was supportive of foxhunting for her husband and children, but she insisted that the children be home by dark. "One time, I got in late," Albert said. "Again, and there'll be no more hunting for you," she said. "I listened."

Melvin said that Jeanette was the only Poe girl that foxhunted, and in addition to Albert and Melvin, Jim and Roger were the only brothers that continued to ride as adults. "Jim liked to hunt, but he wasn't much of a rider," said Melvin. However, Jim enjoyed steeplechasing, and he and wife Dorothy owned a real good horse, Bar Jacket, who Albert trained to win races in the late 1980s. Melvin added that Roger simply didn't get along with horses, but he's the father of Clydetta, an excellent horsewoman who rode in steeplechases, and Ross, who occasionally hunts in Bath County with his wife Trish, a native of Ireland.

What were known as turnout hunts were popular social and sporting activities in Melvin's youth. For turnouts, foxhunters brought their best hounds to a designated meet, usually on Sunday mornings, when it wasn't unusual to have 40 hounds present. At Hume, the meets were at 9:30 to allow spectators to stop off on the way to the service at the Baptist church. "He's gone," was the cry when the fox was released. "These were native foxes," said Melvin. "They knew the territory, no reason for them getting caught."

Turnout hunts weren't competitive, but hound owners obviously enjoyed cheering on their favorite hounds. Melvin purchased a blue-tick hound from construction workers in Washington, where he was an apprentice just prior to World War II. "These guys took me hunting one night in

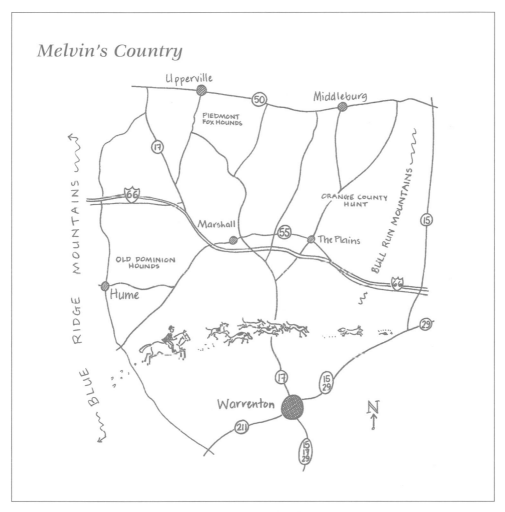

The Old Dominion, Orange County, Warrenton and Piedmont hunts are about 60 miles west of Washington, D.C. in northern Virginia. The Bath County Hounds has a territory about 150 miles distant in west-central Virginia near Hot Springs.

what's now Annandale. This hound, Blue, caught my attention when in full cry in the moonlight down a wood ride. I bought him for $20, which was as much as I made in a week. Blue wasn't the best all-around hound, but he was very fast. On turnouts, he'd burst away from the pack, was the lead hound."

To get foxes for turnouts, Melvin and Albert went hunting equipped with gunnysacks under their saddles and string in their pockets. "After our hounds put a fox to ground, we'd dig him out of his den with a shovel borrowed from the farmer where the den was. When there was two foxes in a den we'd place them in the same sack, tie it in the middle and sling it over our horse's withers. We kept the foxes in a chicken house, but never for more than a week. Otherwise, they'd lose conditioning," Melvin said.

Melvin said that split-rail fences were used on his father's farm, and others. "We cut chestnut tree trunks into eleven foot lengths, then split 'em by working down the trunk with wedges, and made snake fences with the rails. There was no nails, no wire. When I took over as huntsman at Old Dominion after the war, there was still a lot of snake fences in the territory."

Melvin said that Sterling Larrabee, master of his own pack, then Old Dominion in 1930-1940, had very good landowner relations. "He was married to a rich lady and didn't mind spending her money to improve his foxhunting. He paid farmers $5 for every fox found on their farm and $10 for each fox put to ground. Once, his foxhunters jumped a fence into one of our sod fields and cut it up. Mr. Larrabee came around that afternoon after hunting and gave Dad $15. That was serious money, and the foxes-found and gone-to-ground fees added up, encouraged farmers to take good care of their foxes."

Albert Poe often hunted his father's hounds alone, no whips, when Melvin was in the army during the war. "By then, Daddy was hilltopping. Some days I'd ride 20 or more miles to be with hounds. Daddy probably rode five miles, but he knew every den in the countryside and had a sixth sense to be at the right spot when hounds put a fox to ground," Albert said.

Baseball and Jousting

As well as foxhunting, baseball and jousting were important leisure activities in Hume, and the Poes were enthusiastically involved in both.

Baseball was the sole sport at the Hume school. "We were too small to have football and basketball, like the bigger schools in Marshall and

Jousting tournaments have been held in Hume for generations. Melvin, competing as the Knight of Orange County, had his share of championships. Brother Albert was the Knight of Piedmont and daughter Bridgett the Maiden of Ozark.

Warrenton," said Melvin. "We only had 130 or so kids. My graduating class had eight, and six were girls."

Melvin started playing baseball at school by the time he was 10 or 12. "I tinkered with it far earlier, though," he said. "I remember planting corn, poking holes with a stick and throwing in some kernels. Sometimes I'd throw the kernels, pretending I was pitching curve balls."

Melvin progressed from pick-up games to the school team, then on to Hume's town team, showing along the way that he could pitch a good curve ball. He also had a sharp batting eye, could hit curve balls, and he developed a pick-off play that often caught opponents off guard at first base.

When Melvin was stationed in the army in Mississippi, the post's baseball team was mostly composed of professional players that had contracts with major and minor league teams. Melvin tagged along to a game with a buddy who pitched for the team. "That day, they were short a player, and they threw me a uniform," Melvin said. "Amazingly, I got two hits and stuck with the team. This was serious ball. We'd sometimes play in nearby Jackson under lights in a real ballpark."

Hume's baseball team in the 1950s included four foxhunters. Melvin Poe is third from the right in the front row. Carroll Pearson, a whipper-in for Old Dominion, is on Melvin's right and Eddie Pearson, a whipper-in for Cobbler Hunt, on his left. Glen Kines, who has hounds to this day in Hume, is on the far left of the back row.

Following the war, Melvin rejoined Hume's town team. Brother Albert sometimes played as an outfielder for Hume, then switched to Upperville's team after becoming huntsman at Piedmont.

"I think, like wine, I got better as time went on, and, at 36, I played my best ball," Melvin said. "I was the pitcher that year [1956] on Fauquier County's all-star team that played Loudoun [County]. I was shaky early on. They got five hits off me in the first inning, but they didn't score because I picked two men off first base and struck out the other. We blanked 'em that day 5-0."

Melvin quit while he was on top and went on to coach the Hume Hornets, a girl's softball team, for several years. The team mostly consisted of Melvin's daughters, nieces and grand nieces.

Melvin's father and the Chadwells were among many in the county that enjoyed the traditional sport of jousting. "When I was real small, I remember 'em practicing in a meadow on our farm, and in tournaments," Melvin said. Albert claims that jousting was responsible for bringing together their mother and father. "Knights chose maidens as part of the tradition in jousting. That was their first date."

In 1960, Hume's Ruritan Club, in which Melvin was a member, sought a good fundraiser. "We decided on a jousting tournament at the old school grounds, followed by a big supper, and it's been going ever since," Melvin said.

Melvin won his share of tournaments, competing as the Knight of Orange County, while Albert was the Knight of Piedmont and daughter Bridgett the Maiden of Ozark. "One year when Bridgett was the junior champion, she had more rings than any of the adults," Melvin said.

An annual jousting tournament, organized and instructed by Melvin, is part of the Merry Oaks Olympics, hosted for members of the Middleburg Orange County Pony Club by Arthur W. (Nick) Arundel at Merry Oaks Farm, The Plains.

CHAPTER 3

MELVIN'S HUNTS:
OLD DOMINION FOXHOUNDS,
ORANGE COUNTY HUNT AND
BATH COUNTY HOUNDS

MELVIN'S career as a professional huntsman spans more than 50 seasons, with 16 at Old Dominion, 27 with Orange County and 10, and still counting, with Bath County.

Old Dominion

Early on, Sterling Larrabee was solely responsible for good sport in the Old Dominion territory. He loved to hunt and to go hard, but he became discouraged by a dearth of foxes in the 1930s. Larrabee concluded that deer chases would be a way to pick up the slack, but deer, at the time, didn't populate the countryside either. No problem. He contacted a friend in England and had four red deer shipped over—Minnie, Maud, Mabel and Mary—and kept them at the kennel in a lot enclosed by high wire.

Melvin Poe and Orange County's pack of red ring-neck hounds departed from a meet at Salamander Farm in 1989.

Word got around when deer hunts were to be held, and hard riding foxhunters throughout northern Virginia assembled when a deer, carted to the meet, was released. The foxhunters went hell bent for election, the sole rule being that followers weren't to trample the hounds. Following the hunt, the deer was returned to the kennel and rested for another day.

Melvin's army career included the invasion of Normandy. "I was a jeep mechanic, so I was far to the rear of the heavy fighting on D-Day," he said. Always one to accentuate happenings that are fun, Melvin is much more willing to talk about running across kegs of wine in a German village, theirs for the "asking," and his friendship with country music legend Grandpa Jones.

"The wine started what has become a lifelong hobby of making my own wine," Melvin said. "I don't drink it myself, never really enjoyed the taste, but I enjoy giving bottles to my friends." I can assure you that Melvin's home brew can make you rather silly. Ask John Coles, my wine drinking partner in trips to Bath County.

In Europe, Melvin helped Grandpa Jones carry amplifiers and stuff for appearances at service clubs. "Grandpa Jones visited me in Hume following the war when in D.C. for a concert," Melvin said. "I had a picture of the two of us with a favorite hound, but damned if I know what became of it." However, Melvin has a constant reminder of Grandpa Jones, who died 10 or so years ago—Melvin's farm in Hume is named Ozark in honor of the Ozark Regiment, in which Grandpa Jones served in World War II. The Ozark

Regiment was attached to General Patton's Third Army.

By wartime, carted deer hunts were history, and Old Dominion, like other hunts, struggled to provide sport. Shirley Payne, a veteran horseman and foxhunter who was stationed at the Remount Depot at nearby Front Royal, hunted the hounds on weekends. Augustus Riggs IV, later the master of the Howard County Hunt in Maryland, and Carl Schilling of Chicago, were also at Front Royal, and whipped-in to Payne.

Upon discharge from the army, Melvin sought work as a mechanic at local garages. "Luckily, as it turned out, I didn't find anything," he said. "Instead, a neighbor, Phil Triplett, who was friendly with the powers-to-be in the hunt, recommended me for the huntsman's job. I got it for the grand

Melvin Poe had great respect for Col. Albert P. Hinckley, the master of the Old Dominion Hounds, here with Mrs. Hinckley at a meet at Henchmans Lea in 1965.

salary of $90 a month."

Melvin said that he took over a pack of 13 hounds. "I could run faster than 10 of them," he said. "Albert had much better hounds than the hunt club, and he loaned them to the hunt in trade for the use of a hunting horse. One of the hounds, Ollie Poe's Joe, became a foundation sire of Old Dominion's pack. Joe had good breeding—Bywaters blood on his sire's side, out of an Orange County bitch."

Melvin, of course, was intimately familiar with the countryside. " I knew as much about peoples' farms as they did—the lines and boundaries, panels, rocks, dens." And he also had a whipper-in, Carroll Pearson, who Melvin described as the "best foxhunter I've ever seen." Melvin said that Pearson knew every hound's voice. "I could tell which dogs were running; he could tell me, right off, which dogs weren't running."

Melvin also highly respected Col. Albert P. Hinckley, who was Old

Dominion's master in 1947-1968. "He just loved to hunt. If he had 50 [field members] behind him, that was fine. If he had one behind, that was OK too. He just loved the chase, and he had a lot of really good horses. He also had friends at the British embassy in Washington. Many were foxhunters, and he invited them out on weekends."

Several developments came about in the early 1950s that seriously affected foxhunting in northern Virginia. The fox population was decimated by an outbreak of rabies, and deer invaded the area. Melvin's childhood practice of digging foxes from earths was put to use. "We'd go out of our hunting country and pay farmers $5 a fox to let us dig up their foxes," he said. "At one time we had 43 foxes in a chicken pen at Col. Hinckley's. We inoculated them for rabies, dipped them for mange, tagged them, then 'planted' them in groundhog holes. Getting the groundhogs out was simple. They hate fox litter. We put some in the holes and they left in no time. After putting some food and water in with the foxes, we stopped the earths for a couple days. Then we further encouraged them to stay around by placing meat, dog food or chicken parts at the earth."

Melvin said that most of the foxes stayed put, but one of his tagged foxes ended up in Potomac, Maryland, ten years later, killed on a highway. He also said that the importation of foxes from a trapper in Iowa got under way in his days at Old Dominion. "The first lot came by train and sat in their cages on the platform of the rail station at Catlett. That wasn't good because taking foxes across state lines wasn't exactly legal. Later, shipments were made by truck to a farm near Charles Town, West Virginia, where me and other huntsmen picked them up," Melvin said.

Melvin is surprised that few country people can tell the difference between groundhog and fox dens. "Foxes don't dig earths, they move into the ones dug by groundhogs," he said. "You can tell right off who's living there. A groundhog places dirt in piles right outside the den. A fox cleans out his den by scratching dirt back at the entrance, evenly spread, not in piles." Melvin also explained that a groundhog puts an airhole in earths, straight up. "Those are the holes that cause bad falls for foxhunters," he said.

End of "Nature Boy's" class on dens. Back to horse and hound anecdotes, and the old-timers in the Old Dominion country have a favorite. It seems that Col. Hinckley stood the stallion Irish Luck, a good sire of field hunters. One day, a mare owned by a farmer in the hunting country was in heat, and he wanted to breed her to Irish Luck. Melvin, however, was slated to hunt Irish Luck. No problem. On hacking to the meet, Melvin stopped off at the horse breeder's farm, took the tack off Irish Luck, bred him to the mare, then proceeded to the meet. "Old Irish Luck went better than ever that day," Melvin said.

All went well for Melvin and Albert Poe. Melvin showed great sport, and he and his wife Jane had four children, three girls and a boy. Albert, in addition to hunting with Melvin, made green horses for Col. Hinckley and looked after Mrs. Hinckley in the hunting field. He also worked for Phil Triplett, artificially inseminating cows. Triplett had customers in Piedmont's hunting country, and he was aware that Mrs. A. C. Randolph and Paul Mellon, the masters of Piedmont in 1954, needed a huntsman to replace Josh Craun, who retired. "I got the job because I'd been around hounds and hunting all my life and because Melvin was doing so well at Old Dominion," Albert said.

Developments soon occurred, however, that had an immense bearing on Melvin's career, and a lady, Peggy Johnson, was the catalyst. She, husband Ed and daughters Chrissy and Kathy moved from New Jersey to Virginia in the 1950s and bought a farm in the Old Dominion territory. Ed became a director of the hunt and an honorary whipper-in, while Peggy sometimes took the field when Col. Hinckley wasn't out.

"My marriage was in trouble," Peggy said. "I'd married at age 19, in retrospect to escape an unhappy home life. In Virginia, the marriage further went downhill, and we separated. Melvin did his best to make me feel important, needed. He taught me what foxhunting is all about, and we'd often go over and ride Col. Hinckley's young horses. One thing led to another; we'd hunt Tuesdays, Thursdays and Saturdays, and find one reason or another to see each other on the other days."

Peggy and Melvin often met at Thumb Run Church and took a logging trail up into the woods. "I guess I was a challenge for Melvin," said Peggy. "Young. Pretty. Supposedly rich. Available. I remember that we once fantasized that we'd live happily ever after, that he would be the Orange County huntsman and me the whipper-in. I asked, 'Why Orange County?' He replied that Orange County and Piedmont were the best hunts in Virginia, and Albert already had Piedmont."

After 16 years as Old Dominion's huntsman, a change came about that eventually led to making the pie-in-the-sky daydream a reality. Word of their romance got back to Col. Hinckley, who confronted Melvin. Either he quit seeing Peggy or he was fired. Melvin chose the latter, and Hinckley placed an announcement in *The Chronicle of the Horse* that Melvin Poe was no longer associated with the Old Dominion Hounds. "I had a job-wanted ad in the same issue," said Melvin. "I got lots of replies and signed on as a whipper-in for Orange County."

Morton W. (Cappy) Smith (left), the master of the Orange County Hunt in 1971-1979, greets Charles T. Matheson, who became president of the hunt in the 1990s.

Orange County

Melvin embarked upon his job at Orange County on July 1, 1962, joining a hunt with a proud history. It dates to 1900, near Goshen, New York, in Orange County, hence the name. By 1903, though, the New York hunt territory was fighting a losing battle with urbanization, so the hunt's leaders, including E. H. Harriman, father of Gov. Averell Harriman, sought happier hunting grounds in The Plains, Virginia.

The English foxhounds brought to Virginia didn't hunt well, so the New Yorkers enlisted the aid of William Skinker Jr., a native Virginian who sold horses and hunted his own pack of red ring-neck hounds. In 1905, Skinker sold his pack and his 70-acre farm near The Plains to the Orange County Hunt, and he became master and huntsman. To this day, Orange County's kennels are on the original Skinker farm, and red ring-necks are still used.

A rambling clubhouse in The Plains housed the out-of-towners, excepting railroad magnate Harriman, who stayed in a Pullman car on a siding in the village. The Pullman had opulent furnishings; some insist the bathroom fixtures were solid gold. The clubhouse was destroyed in a fire that swept through The Plains in 1968 when a gasoline tank truck collided with a train.

The Orange County Hunt moves off from a meet in 1989. In the foreground (left-right)

are whippers-in Chrissy Gray, Charles B.(Butch) Gray III and huntsman Melvin Poe.

At the kennels, a dormitory housed up to 30 grooms, and two 28-stall horse barns that resembled those at Belmont Park racetrack in New York were available. No question, the New Yorkers went first class, but they were low-key in other ways. Scarlet coats weren't allowed in the hunting field, except for the staff; hunt collars were taboo; hunt balls weren't held. These traditions remain to this day.

The out-of-towners were strictly interested in good hunting and good times, and to further these ends, they secured permission from the masters of the Piedmont Fox Hounds to hunt portions of its vast hunting country. At the time, Piedmont's territory consisted of the entire territories now hunted by the Piedmont, Orange County and Middleburg hunts.

In 1906, Harry Worcester Smith, the master of Piedmont, accused Orange County of overstepping its bounds, that portions of the country not in the agreement were being hunted. Smith sought resolution of the dispute by the National Steeplechase and Hunt Association, then the governing body of both sports, but the NSHA chose not to become involved. Hence, Smith was one of the founders in 1907 of the Masters of Foxhounds Association of America, which in time resolved the dispute. To this day, Segregation Lane, on the boundaries of the two hunts, is a reminder of past problems.

Prominent sportsmen have been associated through the years with the Orange County Hunt. E. H. Harriman's daughter and son-in-law, Mr. and Mrs. R. Penn-Smith, were masters of Orange County in the 1920s. The Penn-Smith daughters, Nancy and Avie, spent their childhood at Whitewood, now the estate of George L. Ohrstrom. Nancy Penn-Smith Hannum has been the master of Mr. Stewart's Cheshire Foxhounds in Pennsylvania since 1949, and she was America's first great female huntsman.

Other famous Orange County foxhunters include Jacqueline Kennedy Onassis, Senator John W. Warner, who served on the hunt's board of stewards, and Paul Mellon, whose home farm, Rokeby, is in the heart of Piedmont's country. To subscribe to Orange County, one must own property in the home country, so to be eligible Mr. Mellon purchased what now is the Virginia Tech Experimental Farm on the road between Middleburg and The Plains.

Fletcher Harper, though, was the one who really put Orange County on the map. Mr. Harper was formerly an amateur steeplechase rider of some note, and he was very organized, attended to every detail. He became master in 1920 and served through 1953, during which time Orange County showed excellent sport, and its hounds were consistent winners at hound shows. Mrs. Harper, the former Harriet Wadsworth, a member of a famed foxhunting family in Geneseo, New York, was a major asset in helping her husband establish Orange County as one of the premier hunts in America.

Mr. Harper appointed Sterling (Duke) Leach to succeed Ned Chadwell as Orange County's huntsman in 1924. Leach was a brilliant huntsman, and he and Fletcher Harper supervised the hound breeding program. However, when Melvin made the scene at Orange County, Leach was nearing 70, and I am told that he was living on his reputation, having lost a lot of his enthusiasm for going hard across country behind his hounds. However, he was reluctant to step down, and, naturally, viewed Melvin as a threat to his job.

Melvin and Peggy were married in 1963, but this wasn't a happy time for the newlyweds. Melvin was hospitalized for a time with acute asthma attacks, which were psychosomatic in nature, in all probability brought on by the effects of a tumultuous divorce and a strained relationship with Duke Leach.

In 1964, Melvin became huntsman, but it was still unpleasant because Leach stayed on for another two years as kennel huntsman, and was, according to Melvin, "much more of a hindrance than a help." Leach sometimes followed the hunt in a truck, and when the pack drew a covert, he would blow his hunting horn to confuse hounds, to encourage them to leave Melvin.

It was Leach, though, who was finally asked to leave, and Melvin prospered under joint-masters Thomas F. Furness, who was originally from the Midwest, and Charles Green Turner, a native Virginian. "Mr. Furness was the nicest man in the world, and Mr. Turner my kind of man," said Melvin. "He was a country person, through and through, had lived in the area forever, and always had his own pack of hounds. He was a real foxhunter, and a character. He had a big, deep voice and was very positive, never dissatisfied, always in a good humor."

The other masters during Melvin's tenure as huntsman were Henry N. Woolman III (1965-1973), Morton W. (Cappy) Smith (1971-1979), William H. (Mike) du Pont (1979-1987), James L. Young (1982-present) and Charles S. Whitehouse (1990-2001). Melvin rates Mike du Pont as the best field master. "He was riding with success in point-to-points at the time, so he was well mounted, and he loved to hunt," Melvin said. He added that Cappy Smith was known the world over in horse circles for his immense success with show hunters, so he attracted a lot of important people and prestige to the hunt, and Jimmy Young even more so as president of the Masters of Foxhounds Association. "Jimmy Young and Mike du Pont were the first masters in my time to take a real interest in breeding hounds and the hound shows," said Melvin.

Leadership, of course, is vitally important, but the success of foxhunting really depends on the availability of good hunting country and good relations between the hunt leaders and members with landowners. Orange County's country is heaven on earth for foxhunters. The majority of the territory—which lies south of Middleburg, east to Aldie, south to The Plains and west

to Atoka Road and Segregation Lane—has small coverts and open, rolling land, mostly used for cattle and horses, with very little cropland. "You can be right with hounds, keep 'em in sight for 50 or 60 percent of the time, instead of maybe 10 percent in Old Dominion's rougher, more wooded country," said Melvin.

According to Dr. Hugh B. Lynn, a longtime foxhunter with a key farm in Orange County's territory, Melvin was like a master in many respects, particularly in landowner relations. "He was in intimate contact with the

The whippers-in for the 1978 season at Orange County included (left-right) Peggy Poe, Chrissy Gray and John Coles. Photographer Marshall Hawkins nicknamed them "The Three Musketeers."

landowners, and everyone liked him, respected him. For years, he was the heart of the Orange County Hunt."

Melvin worked hard to increase Orange County's fox population. "We brought in a good many foxes from the trapper in Iowa. The ones today are the grandchildren or the great grandchildren of foxes we put out years ago," he said.

Melvin once came to the aid of his childhood friend "Buster" Chadwell, the huntsman of the Essex Fox Hounds in New Jersey. "Buster was really short on foxes at the time," Melvin said. "I dug him up a couple grays and threw in two reds, one a vixen, the other a male. He named them Peggy and Melvin. Buster called one night all excited, saying they'd had a hell of a race after Peggy."

Melvin enjoyed his success with family members at his side during much of his years at Orange County. Early on, Peggy rode in the rear of the field, making green horses and giving mileage to horses belonging to clients, or watching out for her customers. (A description of the Poe's bed and breakfast for people and horses is in chapter 4.)

Melvin soon came to depend on Peggy in the hunting field. "He'd sometimes ask me to ride out and see what was going on, or to knock off hounds," she said. In 1970, Peggy became a full-time professional member of the staff. "I'll never forget her first day [as a whip]," Melvin said. "She was standing on a hill and all sorts of fussing was going on. I went up to see what it was all about. 'He's right down there, down there,' she stammered. I asked what's down there. 'The fox, the fox,' she managed to say. 'Well, why in the hell didn't you just say so,' I asked."

This prompted Peggy to develop a scream when viewing foxes away. "It got so that you could hear her all over the countryside, and hounds came to hark to her scream," Melvin said. Believe me, Peggy's patented "gone away" screams will raise your hackles. I hear them to this day in Bath County, where Peggy follows the hunt in the hound truck.

At Orange County, the family fun picked up a notch in 1978, when Peggy's daughter Chrissy became a whipper-in. Chrissy showed ponies as a kid and was active in the Middleburg Orange County Pony Club. She was a natural rider and started hunting as a child, and in time, just as in Peggy's case, Melvin asked Chrissy to ride ahead or on the flank, and she and contemporaries Jonathan Lynn and Gould Brittle became junior whips. "I remember George Ohrstrom [president of the hunt] telling me, 'Don't ever let young people get disinterested in the hunt,'" Melvin said.

Following graduation from high school, Chrissy became a professional staff member. In addition to whipping-in, she took care of the hunt horses. "It wasn't like a job in those days, just fun," she said. Chrissy's sister, Kathy, also followed in the Poe tradition by being a whip for two seasons at Old Dominion, and she's now the field master of their hilltopper's field.

Melvin said that Chrissy, like Peggy, had a sixth sense to be in the right spot at the right time. "She never screamed like Peggy, but had a good loud 'tally-ho.'" Melvin added that Peggy has a bum neck, has trouble turning her head to the left. "As a result, Peggy always whipped-in on the left side, Chrissy on the right."

Melvin, Peggy and Chrissy made a great team. However, incidents during a hunt in 1980 sidelined two of the team and led to the retirement of a third member. "We were on a real good chase near Delaplane when my horse fell in a groundhog hole," Melvin said. "Chrissy was galloping at my side. When I went down, her horse spooked, lunged abruptly and Chrissy flew off." Melvin was unconscious and Chrissy couldn't get up, having landed on her knees. A field member pulled Melvin into sitting position, and the hound, Westwood, licked blood from his face.

Peggy was several hills distant doing her whipping thing when this happened. "I heard sirens, and when I came a hill closer, I saw two of the four pink coats that were out that day. Uh, oh, I thought, I hope the two missing ones don't belong to me."

Melvin had a broken nose and severely wrenched neck. Chrissy's problem was more like a knock on a funny bone, no real damage. Westwood had to be restrained from joining them in the ambulance. John Coles, also whipping, picked up the pack and filled in as huntsman for Melvin for the following six weeks.

Photographer Marshall Hawkins was in action on the day of the falls, and recorded the happenings. "He had it all, frame after frame with one of those cameras with a motor, right from the approach of the fox down to Westwood licking Melvin's face and trying to get into the ambulance. Marshall wondered why we didn't want any of his pictures," Peggy said.

For some time, Peggy had worried about Melvin getting hurt. "This fall really unnerved me," she said. "I knew that Melvin would never stop, and I never asked him to, but the time had come for me to quit."

Melvin and Peggy's daughter, Bridgett, in junior high at the time, was aware of her mother's feelings. A poem she wrote hangs in the Poe's living room:

The Huntsman's Daughter to the Huntsman's Wife

He glides across the open fields,
The thought is always there.
With flowing tones of cunning sport,
He sometimes loses care.

He gallops along the barren woods,
The stone wall meets his way.
He maneuvers all the obstacles,
To aid the sporting day.

The chase is on, the risk is there,
The excitement begins to rise.
The pace quickens, his voice is heard,
To mark the fox to ground.

Yes, the risks are real, the price is high,
But fulfillment is also there.
It's his way of life, he needs his sport,
As well as the assurance of you.

Bridgett Lee Poe, December 1980

The fall was one of many through the years for Melvin, in and out of the hunting field. He once broke some ribs while rushing to change TV channels for a football game, and he sustained injuries after falling from a roof and when a tree fell on his leg during trail clearing. "It got that I hated once more to call the masters and tell them that their man was sidelined," said Peggy.

Charles B. (Butch) Gray III, a member of a Virginia family long associated with foxhunting, was a professional whip for Orange County, and he became Chrissy's husband. "Butch was as good a whip as I've ever had," said Melvin. "He and Chrissy were a great team."

During the 1990-1991 season, with Melvin just shy of his seventieth birthday, the masters determined that the time had come to retire their huntsman. A final meet with Melvin carrying the horn was carded at Tom Carroll's farm in late March 1991.

"It was the best day of my life," said Melvin. "People came from all over. We jumped a fox right off and had a good run towards Middleburg before going to ground. A little further, we jumped another. The same all day. In all, we accounted for six foxes."

Jimmy Young asked Vicky and Skip Crawford, longtime foxhunters with the Potomac Hunt in Maryland and now two of the joint-masters, to be Orange County's guests on the farewell hunt. Potomac and Orange County have been wonderful rivals at hound shows for years, and the members of the two hunts have mutual respect and friendship. "Skip couldn't get away from work, so Camille, our teenage daughter, and I came down," said Vicky. "Wow. It was incredible, a five-star day in anybody's book. Everything fell into place. It was all about Melvin."

On the way back to the meet, Melvin and his staff and what remained of the field had to jump a fairly large coop rather then asking their tired horses to face a lengthy detour. "It was the only time in my life that I was thoughtful about a fence," said Melvin. "I thought about a soldier getting killed after peace was declared, of a football player getting hurt after victory was in the bag, but we all got over just fine."

After stepping down, Melvin was kennel huntsman for two years. "These were the worst years of my life," he said. "Butch took over as hunts-man, but this simply didn't work out, and he was let go after one season. This was a big blow to me. I hated to have my man not work out. I feared for the future of my hounds, of my hunt country. I was miserable."

Mark Stickley (1992-1997) and Mark Cassidy (1997-2000) followed Butch Gray. Adrian Smith became the huntsman in the 2000-2001 season. Gray became the huntsman at Piedmont in 2001.

John Coles, who became a joint-master at Orange County in 2001, says that Melvin continues to be a big help in hunting matters. "He's the guy I go to when I need advice," John said.

Bath County

George Ohrstrom, a longtime president of the Orange County Hunt and a great admirer of the Poes, came up with a perfect solution for getting Melvin's thoughts away from the awkward transitions at Orange County. Melvin would be the huntsman of a start-up hunt in Bath County, a 3½-hour drive from Hume and George's home farm at The Plains.

In the early 1980s, George purchased Fassifern Farm at Warm Springs, nine miles from The Homestead, the famed resort hotel. An inn on the present site of The Homestead dates back to 1846, the "modern" Homestead to 1890.

The Jackson River, which has some of Virginia's finest trout fishing, runs through Fassifern, which is named for a town in Scotland, the birthplace of the first owner. Open, rolling pastures are on either side of the river, with mountains and national forests forming backdrops on both sides of the valley. This results in lovely views, as pretty land as you'd ever care to see.

Fay Ingalls, the owner of The Homestead, gave an eloquent description of the area in his book *The Valley Road, The Story of Virginia Hot Springs*. "For more than half a century I have known and loved that portion of the higher Allegheny Mountains which comprises the counties of Bath and Highland in Virginia and the neighboring ones across the line in West Virginia. Although there are rugged peaks and deep ravines, it is essentially a peaceful, gentle land. The landscape has a feminine charm, with its high hills, buttressed by rounded shoulders, sweeping smoothly down to the valleys. It bespeaks of fertility and life, with its wooded hillsides overlooking green pastures."

Over the years, George Ohrstrom has accumulated additional farmland in this marvelous area, and now owns over 3,000 acres on a four-mile stretch of the Jackson River.

Bath County has a proud sporting heritage. Turkey, bear and deer hunting are important pastimes in addition to angling, and foxhunting has long been enjoyed. In the late 1800s, Tate Sterrett kept a pack of foxhounds at Fassifern and organized the Fassifern Hunt Club. Carriages brought spectators and participants to Fassifern from The Homestead for an annual horse show and race meet. The climax of the day was a point-to-point in which entrants dashed across the Jackson River.

Rachel Ingalls (Fay's wife) founded the Bath County Hunt in 1932, and the Masters of Foxhounds Association recognized her hunt two years later. Mrs. Ingalls hunted a drag pack, and Cecil Tuke and W. Burling Cocks, who became a Hall of Fame steeplechase trainer, alternated as huntsmen of a pack that hunted live. Under Cocks' leadership a steeplechase race meet sanctioned by the National Steeplechase and Hunt Association was held on land adjacent to Fassifern in 1936.

The 1939 Hunt Roster issue of the *Middleburg Chronicle* listed Bath County's capping fee at $2.00 and that field hunters could be jobbed from The Homestead for $10.00. The hunt's territory was described: "Rough foxhunting country approximately 17 by 5 miles, mountainous, rocky and steep, with many gray foxes, some reds. Beautiful drag country with natural rail fences, post-and-rail panels, logs and ditches."

The Homestead ran an advertisement in the September 1933 issue of *The Sportsman* magazine. Under a sketch of a foxhunter over a huge post-and-rail fence, the text read: "Why go abroad for the hunt or 'the cure?' Indeed, why go at all when there's The Homestead with its beautiful cool

mountains, 100 horses, live fox and drag hunts thrice weekly, skeet, golf and tennis! Ask your doctor about 'the cure.' Direct train service to Hot Springs, Virginia, with air conditioned Pullmans." I am told that the officials of the Masters of Foxhounds Association looked with askance at the ad, feeling that it commercialized the sport of foxhunting.

Foxhunting lapsed in Bath County during World War II, and the hunt was not activated following the war. The Homestead, however, became the host of the Bath County National Horse Show and competitive trail rides. Each August in 1928 through 1966, the A-rated show was one of the most popular on the circuit. Its demise came when major show stables opted to attend shows that were more accessible, and more economical. Tommy Lee Jones's experience in 1962 is an example. He rode Cheyenne to be the open jumper champion. His truck, however, blew a gasket in ascending Warm

Foxhunting in Bath County, near Hot Springs in west central Virginia, has a long heritage. Followers of the Fassifern Hunt Club, circa 1907, are in front of the farmhouse on the property now owned by George L. Ohrstrom. The Bath County Hunt was in operation in the area in 1932-1941. The Bath County Hounds, under Mr. Ohrstrom's leadership, enjoyed its tenth year of sport in 2001.

Springs Mountain. "The repairs equaled the prize money," he said.

Attempts to revive the show in 1992 and 1993 failed. Competitive trail rides, on the other hand, continue in the spring and fall to this day over a vast trail system developed by The Homestead. The late Paul Mellon competed in the 100-mile ride 17 times between 1959 and 1979 and was a five-time winner, the final time at age 71.

Aware of Bath County's sporting heritage, George Ohrstrom hit upon the idea of reviving foxhunting in the area. John Coles, who was in charge of real estate and farm management matters for George, took Melvin and Peggy to Bath County in the late summer of 1992, and they saw potential for sport. This prompted George to share his plans for foxhunting with Mr. and Mrs. Philip R. Hirsh, the owners of neighboring Meadow Lane, a 1,600-acre farm with a commercial lodge that is popular with anglers, bird watchers and nature lovers. The ruins of Fort Dinwiddie, which was built in 1755 under George Washington's orders as protection against Indian attacks, are on a bluff at Meadow Lane overlooking the Jackson River. The George Washington National Forest and the Hidden Valley Camp Grounds are Meadow Lane's neighbors to the north.

The first meet of the Bath County Hounds was at Meadow Lane Lodge on Thursday, October 15, 1992, with a field of 12 foxhunters and a large number of the curious. Some of the onlookers were old timers from the days of the original hunt; many were owners of bear hounds, thus curious to see how the "fancy" foxhunters operated; and a number of the guests at the Lodge enjoyed the spectacle.

Appropriately, hounds immediately found a red fox in a patch of under-growth near the banks of the Jackson River. The entourage viewed the fox across a meadow, but they had to look quickly as the fox soon went to ground. Notes in my hunting diary describe the fun: "Country not hunted by a pack of foxhounds for 49 years, since the disbanding of the Bath County Hunt. Busy morning. Found three foxes in Meadow Lane's mountain valley. One nice view. Foxes tend to run from open bottomlands up into mountains on either side of valley. Lovely fall color. Great time. Melvin hunted eight couple red ring-neck hounds 'borrowed' from the Orange County Hunt for this 'experiment.'"

The meet was at Fassifern early the following morning, with heavy mist and mild temperatures. The pack opened with extreme enthusiasm on a line that originated in a cow pasture near a deer carcass. Hounds crossed the Jackson River in full cry, up sheer cliffs on the far side, then shut down, bam. "That wasn't a fox or deer, I know that from the dogs' cry, they were some kind of excited," Melvin said later. "Must have been a bear or bobcat. The dogs sure lost interest in a hurry."

Later in the day, hounds surprised a fox in a covert on the Dunn farm and found another on Ohrstrom's Folly Farm, three or four miles west of Fassifern. The "experiment" was deemed a success, and plans were afoot for a renewal of foxhunting in Bath County on a regular basis.

Orange County's masters were extremely supportive, drafting eight couple of elderly, steady hounds to the fledgling hunt. Construction was soon under way on a small kennel at Melvin's farm in Hume, the year-round home of the pack, and runs were enlarged at an existing dog kennel at

Huntsman Melvin Poe called hounds at Bath County in 1994.

Fassifern for visits to Bath County.

In 1993, seven visits were carded, from August through mid-November. Typically, we departed northern Virginia at noon on Wednesday, spent the night at the rambling farmhouse at Fassifern, while our horses stayed at a converted cow barn on the farm. We hunted Thursday and Friday, and returned home late that afternoon. Guests, mostly Orange County and Old Dominion foxhunters, were invited, and Bath County natives were encouraged to hunt. The natives were mostly involved in competitive trail riding, but some competed in hunter shows. Few had previously hunted. The average field for the private hunt was less than ten. John Coles whipped to Melvin, sometimes accompanied by his children—Fraley, Peyton and Sloane.

Melvin soon realized that the Bath County territory, though unsurpassed in beauty, offers unique challenges. In addition to the rugged territory, which makes it difficult to view and hear hounds, the soil base is shaley, not the best for holding scent. More important, though, is that we were definitely spoiled by the abundance of foxes during the "experiment." A serious shortage, on the other hand, was the rule during the first seasons. The fox, it seems, is generally considered expendable in Bath County because he's accused of killing young turkeys, and turkey hunting is vitally important in the area. As a result, foxes are commonly shot or trapped.

The Ohrstrom farms, as well as Meadow Lane and the neighboring Patrick Haynes farm (wife Bebe and the five Haynes children are enthusiastic

— 49 —

foxhunters) are posted. This totals over 5,000 acres. In 1994, a year-round fox feeding program was under way on these properties. As a result, the fox population has increased.

A review of the 1996 season in *The Chronicle of the Horse* indicated the turnaround: "The quality of sport has been greatly improved by a fox feeding program, and a number of gates and panels have been built. Neighboring hunts in the Shenandoah Valley, the Rockbridge and Glenmore, hunted with us this season. The day in early October with Rockbridge was easily the best of the season. Hounds found a big red fox nicknamed Clyde, for the farmer who heads the feeding program. Clyde gave 30 followers a one-hour race in open bottomland. Clyde was also in good form for Glenmore's guests in late October, this time going to ground after about 30 minutes."

Glenmore Hunt's newsletter reported: "Hunting behind the legendary huntsman Melvin Poe was great. He didn't need a whipper-in. His hounds don't know what a deer is. All stayed within close range unless on a line. Great to see. And the field viewed the fox and had a great run."

What has become known as "The Great Bear Hunt" was one of the highlights of the 1997 season. As you'll discover, it really wasn't a great hunt, but bears have always been a big thing with Melvin, and he enjoys telling stories of the trapping of bears by the animal welfare people in the Hume area, and of taking them to Bath County to turn them loose.

Chalker Kansteiner, 10, was the horn blower for a day of hunting at Bath County in 2000.

One day in early October, hounds drew a field of standing corn at Meadow Lane, just below Fort Dinwiddie. It was blank, but Melvin noted that considerable damage had been done in parts of the corn. "Looks like a tank went through. A bear, I'll bet anything, and a big one," he said. Several farmers in the area reported similar damage, which resulted in a night hunt with bear hounds, but the bear wasn't around.

The joint meet with our friends from Rockbridge in October was a slow day until hounds drew a cornfield at Upper Fassifern. A hound spoke, others opened, and something big crashed out of the corn. David Connor, the hunts-man of Rockbridge, was on one side of the cornfield with Melvin. "It was big and black, I thought it was a cow," David said. Melvin and David stopped hounds just before the bear descended a cliff bordering a highway frequently used by logging trucks.

The size of the bear increased as the day went on, as when foxhunters exaggerate the size of fences and the length of runs. Melvin first rated the bear at 300 pounds, but he grew to 500 pounds at the hunt breakfast. Melvin later said, "You don't see bears that big in zoos." And, of course, there was speculation as to whether the bear originally hailed from Hume.

Visits by legendary huntsmen Tommy Lee Jones and Albert Poe were among the highlights of the 2001 season. Both are great company and story-tellers, and were a big help whipping to Melvin in the absence of John Coles, who was sidelined with an injured foot.

Tommy Lee, now in his thirty-second year as huntsman for the Casanova (Va.) Hunt, is distantly related to Melvin, their pedigrees tracing to the Pearson family of Hume. Tommy Lee wrote in Bath County's guest book: "It's great to hunt once more behind the master huntsman." He added that it had been all too long since he'd had the privilege, back to Melvin's days at Orange County.

Albert enjoyed hunting with hounds that he had given Melvin upon disbanding his own private pack at the end of the prior season. Through the years, the brothers had rarely hunted together. Albert said: "I'd hunted behind Melvin several times at Orange County and with Bath County's hounds in the country around Hume, but Melvin has never been out when I hunted hounds." Albert reminisced about a hunt on Christmas Eve in the mid-1970s, though, when the hounds of the brothers inadvertently joined forces. At the time, he was huntsman for Piedmont and Melvin for Orange County. "Our packs managed to jointly put a fox to ground," Albert said. "I whipped my hounds off in Orange County's territory near Segregation Lane, with Orange County's followers on one side of a multi-flora hedge, Piedmont's on the other. We gathered our hounds, wished each other Merry Christmas and went our ways."

I'm certain that some wonder why Bath County's loyal followers from northern Virginia subject themselves to long trips to Bath County year after year when they could stay home and most likely have superior hunting.

There are lots of reasons.

Obviously, there's the beauty of the valleys in the Allegheny Mountains at the best time of year, and the privilege of riding in the pocket of a great huntsman, and at day's end to hear his explanations of all that transpired. Is there a better way to learn what hunting is all about?

Then, there are intangibles. There's the charisma, charm and enthusiasm of Melvin and Peggy (the best cook ever), and the camaraderie of fellow guests, especially children who have played hookey from school for a field trip to Bath County with their parents. I remember Sloane Coles, at age five on her pony Oil Can Harry, being led in the hunting field by her mother Julie, on foot. Several years later, Sloane galloped helter-skelter all over the countryside like an Indian whipping to Melvin. Today, she's one of the most accomplished juniors in horse showing in the United States.

I remember, too, a day when Melvin was under the weather and couldn't hunt the hounds. No problem. John Coles stepped up, but there was a problem because John can only blow a reed horn, not Melvin's conventional horn. After breakfast, Melvin passed his horn around to see who would ride with John as the official horn blower. The adults huffed and puffed, and failed, while Chalker Kansteiner, 10, picked up the horn and almost blew us out of the kitchen. Do you think Chalker will ever forget his day as the huntsman's horn blower?

I also love the extra-curricular activities in Bath County, like relaxing in the baths at Warm Springs after hunting, in the bathing house that dates to 1761. Thomas Jefferson visited Warm Springs in 1781, and bathed in the springs three times a day. According to an advertising flyer of The Homestead, Jefferson described the waters as being "of the first merit." In his honor, the baths are named the Jefferson Pools. The structure of the bathhouse has not changed through the years other than to put new boards in place for ones that have given way.

Then too, croquet tournaments organized by Melvin in the early evenings at Fassifern are always fun, and sometimes controversial. John Coles and I insist that Poe alters the rules to suit his game, and teasingly accuse him of using "Hume rules." Albert explained during his visit that croquet has long been a family pastime. "My grandmother [Florence Pearson] loved croquet and frequently had games on Sundays on the lawn of her farm near Hume," he said.

And, of course, after-dinner sips of Melvin's wine are mandatory for everyone but Melvin, the perfect way to end the day.

Melvin Poe concentrates on a shot during a croquet game, which is a traditional activity in late afternoons at Fassifern Farm, Bath County, Virginia.

CHAPTER 4

SOME OF MELVIN AND PEGGY'S OTHER ACTIVITIES: WINE, PEOPLE AND PIGS, MOVIES AND MINIS

BACK IN the late 1960s, the Poe family had a monopoly of sorts on Hume's female population, Bridgett and Patti having joined half-sisters Chrissy and Kathy. The population growth prompted various ways to provide additional income and activities at Ozark Farm.

Melvin raised cattle, made hay and attended to a myriad of chores associated with a 70-acre farm. In addition to playing baseball and competing in jousting tournaments, his hobbies included making wine and passing his home brew to friends, particularly after long days of hunting. His wine received international acclaim in 1991, when Michael Clayton, the editor of England's leading hunting journal, *Horse and Hound*, had a day with Orange County and wrote of the sport in his magazine. Melvin's picture was on the cover of that issue. Clayton wrote: "The genial Mr. Poe is shown on our cover

In 1979, Melvin was the star in the film documentary Thoughts on Foxhunting.
He poses with his hounds for a picture taken by the producer, Davenport Films,
to promote the film.

carrying two bottles, which are not commercial brands of liquor. The bottles contain his own brew, known as Fox Wine, in sweet or dry versions. I found it very refreshing."

Back in the early days of marriage, Peggy was in charge of the horses and ponies, and, between babies, she broke two colts for a neighbor, Tom Simmons. She started the young horses in the hunting field, and they eventually raced in point-to-points, trained by Peggy. Both had the distinction of falling in their first starts with respective jockeys Tommy Skiffington and Jerry Fishback. Novices at the time, Skiffington and Fishback became national jockey champions.

Peggy also was the huntsman for the Middleburg Orange County Pony Club's pack of beagles. The hunt, founded in 1961 by Eve Fout, provides fun on Thursdays and Sundays during the season for children, mounted, in the territories of the Middleburg and Orange County hunts. The beagles turn up their noses at rabbits, hunting foxes instead. "Hank" Woolman, formerly the master of Orange County, and Hubert Davy are now the huntsmen.

The Bed and Breakfast

When school segregation ceased in the 1960s, Melvin and Peggy purchased the neighboring two small buildings and an acre of land formerly used as the school for Hume's black children. Melvin converted the two structures into hunt boxes, each with two bedrooms, a living room and kitchen.

John Ireys of Hollywood, California, rented one of the hunt boxes year-round for seven years, and boarded two horses. Ireys had poor vision, so Chrissy, when available, was his babysitter in the hunting field, pointing out the approach of fences and what have you. An embarrassing incident motivated the end of the hunting career of Ireys, who was extremely sensitive. He loaded his hunter, Alice, in a trailer for a day with the Blue Ridge Hunt. He wasn't aware that the trailer jumped off the ball when pulling off. Peggy called ahead to Leon Warner's farm, the site of the meet, to assure Ireys that Alice was all right. Upon arrival, fellow foxhunters greeted Ireys with good-natured jests such as "Great to see you, John, hurry and unload, we're going to have fun." Peggy said that Ireys, mortified, departed for Hollywood shortly after the incident and didn't reappear.

Other boarders at the Poe bed and breakfast through the years included Max Lammers, who hunted with Chagrin Valley Hunt in Ohio, Bob Chuckrow (Rombout Hunt in New York), Michael Flanigan (Arapahoe Hunt in Colorado), Paul Wolk and wife Sheila (Genesee Valley Hunt in New York),

Lee McGettigan (Genesee Valley) and Stewart Marr (Rombout). The Poes also started Zohar Ben-Dov in foxhunting in Virginia. Ben-Dov, who formerly hunted with Rombout, is now an ardent foxhunter with Orange County and Piedmont. His Kinross Farm is in Orange County's territory; his steeplechase horses win important races throughout the United States.

The B&B gained international status with visits from Michael Dempsey, master and huntsman of the Galway Blazers in Ireland, and Willie Leahy, field master. Dempsey hunted behind Melvin at Orange County, and became so impressed that he named a horse after Melvin. "The man fascinated me," said Dempsey. "He cheered on his hounds with a scratchy voice that resembled the screech of a wild bird. I hope the race horse, Melvin Poe, is as enthusiastic." As it turned out, though, Melvin Poe, the horse, lacked speed in point-to-points.

Peggy Johnson (later Poe) plays with daughters Chrissy (left) and Kathy. All three went on to important roles in foxhunting, Peggy and Chrissy as whippers-in with the Orange County Hunt and Kathy as a whipper-in with the Old Dominion Hounds, then field master of that hunt's hilltopper field.

Dr. and Mrs. Hugh Lynn and their children Mikie (Michael Anne), Jonathan and Bailey were particular favorites of the Poes, and vice versa. Mrs. Lynn had known Peggy and her former husband in New Jersey, so she looked up Peggy when visiting in Virginia. At the time, Mikie, 16, saw Chrissy and Kathy schooling their ponies over logs in the front paddock. The three girls hit it off immediately, and Mikie accepted an invitation to stay for a week. It was such fun, though, that she stayed a month.

Jonathan, meanwhile, wanted no part of joining the girls. The following year, however, he was along when Dr. and Mrs. Lynn dropped off Mikie at the Poes for a summer of riding and Pony Club activities. "Jonathan started talking to Melvin," said Dr. Lynn. "Shortly, they sat on a fence, and Melvin showed him how to crack a whip. 'Ever done this?' I heard Melvin say." Hooked by Melvin's charm, Jonathan stayed for the summer.

At summer's end, Mikie and Jonathan returned to Rochester, Minnesota, where their father was head of pediatric surgery at the Mayo Clinic. The children were accompanied by three foxhounds—Theo, a Piedmont hound named for Theo Randolph, master of Piedmont; Peggy, named for you know who; and Klea, named for the wife of the head of surgery at Mayo. The hounds joined two collies and two mutts to form Mikie and Jonathan's pack of hounds.

Dr. and Mrs. Lynn purchased Stonehedge Farm in the heart of the Orange County territory, and enjoyed many seasons of hunting behind Melvin. Jonathan whipped to Melvin on weekends while attending law school at Washington and Lee. Today, he is the Commonwealth Attorney for Fauquier County, Virginia, while Mikie is the director of the Stonewall Jackson Museum, Strasburg, Virginia.

Movie Time

The National Endowment for the Arts had gotten under way in the 1960s, and its administrators were open for ideas for films on local culture. Tom Davenport, who with wife Mimi operates Davenport Films, Delaplane, Virginia, proposed a film on point-to-point racing that received favorable reaction from the Endowment, and additional funding from Paul Mellon. However, when Davenport started interviewing the principals of the sport, he concluded that the subject wouldn't work for what he had in mind. His friend Harrison O'Connor, then a reporter for a county newspaper, suggested foxhunting, focusing on Melvin Poe.

"I visited Melvin at the Orange County kennels," said Davenport. "He was skinning a dead horse while drinking a Pepsi. The kennels looked like

FOXFORD IN AMERICA
hunting with the senior huntsman Melvin Poe of the Orange County

MELVIN POE - DON'T-YA-KNOW

9 770018 514028

Orange County Huntsman, Melvin Poe
Had a horse exceedingly slow!
He was past in the chase
By the Master's full pace
But was first at the kill - Don't-Ya-Know

All Foxhunting Gents say it's so
The Dean of Huntsmen is Poe
On Horse, Horn and Hounds
Mel's knowledge ABOUNDS
And he invented the Fox - Don't-Ya-Know

Winemaker supreme is Poe
A sip will tell you it's so!
His products' Renound
For making you sound
After a fall from your mount - Don't-Ya-Know

Melvin Poe and his home-brewed wine made the cover of Horse and Hound, *England's leading sporting weekly. Michael Clayton, editor, sampled the wine after a day of hunting in 1991. "I find it very refreshing," he wrote.*

Orange County Brian '76 is one of Melvin's
all-time favorite hounds. "He was champion
at the Virginia and Bryn Mawr shows, great
in the field, and he sired champions," Melvin
said. Avid hunters Charley Matheson, Jack
Cheatham, Mike du Pont and Leff Lefferts
commissioned Wally Nall to paint Brian.
They gave Melvin the portrait in 1980.

The painting of Melvin Poe and the Orange
County pack by Wally Nall is in the collection
of Mrs. C. Oliver Iselin III.

Upon disbanding his private pack, Albert Poe gave his hounds and one of his hunters to Melvin. The hounds go back in breeding to the Piedmont and Middleburg kennels. Several of Albert's hounds are in the hound truck following sport at Bath County in 2001. DOUGLAS LEES PHOTO

Above Right:
Mr. and Mrs. George L. Ohrstrom enjoyed a day of hunting in 2001 with the Bath County Hounds, which Mr. Ohrstrom founded in 1992.
DOUGLAS LEES PHOTO

The hunter stable at George Ohrstrom's Fassifern Farm and a part of the George Washington National Forest are backdrops for Melvin Poe and the Bath County pack.
GINY HUNTER PHOTO

Melvin Poe walked his pack from the kennel at Hume in 1998, at which time the majority of Bath County's hounds were red ring-necks drafted from the Orange County Hunt. JANET HITCHEN PHOTO

Albert and Melvin Poe, who hunted together at Bath County in 2001, have a wealth of experience. Albert (left) was the huntsman at Piedmont for 20 seasons, then four years at Fairfax and 15 at Middleburg. Melvin hunted the hounds at Old Dominion for 16 seasons, followed by 27 seasons at Orange County. In 2001, he completed his tenth year as huntsman at Bath County.
JOHN COLES PHOTO

Melvin Poe and Orange County's pack of red ring-neck hounds moved off from a meet at Salamander Farm, The Plains, Virginia, in 1989. Whipper-in Chrissy Gary is in the background. DOUGLAS LEES PHOTO

Melvin's happiness is the result of winning a croquet tournament for foxhunters at Fassifern Farm. Croquet has long been a tradition for members of the Poe family. DOUGLAS LEES PHOTO

Africa, with parts of animals in the runs for dogs to eat. I was fascinated, too, by Melvin's high-pitched voice, and immediately concluded that he was a truly interesting character, more so than the point-to-point types I'd spoken with. I felt that I'd be turned down if the film were just on the hunt. Masters tend to be frightened by the media, but they couldn't refuse if it were on Melvin."

When in high school, Davenport remembered seeing Peggy in the town of Marshall. "She was a knockout, a gorgeous woman, very athletic, pretty, outdoorsy, the type about which teenagers fantasize. I thought she'd be a big asset in the film. In fact, I suggested that the film focus on Peggy and Melvin's romance, but I was turned down, cold, by the Poes."

The documentary was two years in the making, with Davenport receiving help from O'Connor and Catherine Hartz, who filmed several segments while mounted on her hunter. "Watching and filming foxhunting affects you like watching some pageant," Davenport said. "It has a tremendous look to it, and it's exceedingly challenging because there are so many obstacles. It presents something that is very, very old and wonderful, and primitive and powerful."

Davenport sought a theme to tie the film together. Albert Poe suggested that he read Peter Beckford's book *Thoughts on Hunting*, written in England in 1781. It's the bible of the foxhunting world, in print to this day. "Here's a book that says it like it really is," said Albert.

Davenport chose a number of passages from Beckford that described the segments captured on film. "We needed a suitable person to recite the passages," he said. "We concluded that Alexander Mackay-Smith was ideal. He was well known and highly respected, and he was in great contrast to Melvin, with his dry New England accent. Also, he wanted to do it."

Melvin's wonderful yell is heard throughout the film, the hounds and the foxhunters going to him. "That yell, I guess that's how he got me," said Peggy in the film, which was appropriately titled *Thoughts on Foxhunting*.

The concluding scene, in the snow, is truly dramatic. "Harrison's a veteran game hunter," said Davenport. "He built a blind, and Melvin gave him a horse's leg. Sure enough, the fox came padding up, and Harrison got some terribly beautiful footage in the early evening light. We later inserted Melvin's call."

The premier of *Thoughts on Foxhunting* was at the Kennedy Center. "The Poes were there, full strength," said Melvin. "We were some kind of dressed up." The first showing of the film locally was at the Middleburg Community Center. "This was the social event," said Davenport. "Evening scarlet, champagne, dinners before, the works."

Portia, the brood sow of Peggy and Melvin's abortive venture in breeding and selling pot-bellied pigs in the 1980s, was accustomed to living in the house. In boredom, she sometimes opened the refrigerator, and she took pots and pans out of the closet. The Poes warned prospective guests at their bed and breakfast that they would share the house with a pig.

Little Pigs and Little Horses

Potbellied pigs were quite the craze in the 1980s. Peggy bought Portia, a pig the size of a basset, from the zoo at Natural Bridge, Virginia. "Melvin was furious and didn't speak to me for ten days," she said. "In addition to being my brood sow, Portia was a house pig. To control her size, I'd take her outside three times a day. Inside, she tended to get bored. She learned to open the refrigerator, and she sometimes took pots and pans out of the closet. Once, she ate a Brillo pad. I had to warn the B & B guests that there'd be a pig in the house."

The market for potbellied pigs died suddenly in the late 1980s. "The craze was over. People just didn't put them on proper diets, and they got too big for pets. Portia's daughter, Pearl, whom I sold to Margaret White [a longtime foxhunter with Orange County] is still alive but as big as a house," Peggy said.

Peggy ran an ad in the county newspaper at Christmas time for potbellied pigs at near giveaway prices. "Not a single call," she said. "I put Portia and a number of piglets in Melvin's truck and took them back to Natural Bridge."

In the early 1990s, Peggy and Melvin saw a piece on miniature horses on the TV show *Exotic Animals*. They felt that breeding and raising minis—maximum size 34"—would be a piece of cake, what with their experience and knowledge of horses.

In contrast to the pigs, Melvin was enthusiastic about this venture. They bought two in-foal mares in New York for $8,200, and foaled a filly and a colt. They sold the colt at auction for $700, but discovered the mares and the filly had little value to serious breeders because they were registered in only one of the two existing mini breed registries. After several years in the business, the Poes started buying stock from a reputable breeder in North Carolina. They now have three stallions and fifteen mares, and sell weanlings for an average price of $800 for colts, $2,500 for fillies under the name Poe's Petites.

"The market for minis is 50 percent serious breeders, 50 percent pet buyers," said Peggy. "We sell mostly on the Internet [www.poespetites.com] on a page that's designed and updated by daughter Patti and her husband Pat, who are computer whizzes. We find this far better than advertising in the magazines for minis."

By 1993, when foxhunting became a reality in Bath County, the Poes let go of their B & B. "With being away so often, especially in the height of the hunting season, we just couldn't run it properly. Instead, we rent the houses. Now, the minis are very important to us, we work hard at it," Peggy said.

The Poes are important breeders of miniature horses. They stand three stallions and have 15 brood mares at their farm in Hume, Virginia, and sell the offspring through the Internet under the stable name Poe's Petites.

could get away from fighters. For further privacy, the porches had some compartments."

The beds inside the houses were 2½' off cement floors, so hounds could go under the beds or on them. The beds were hinged, and swung up for cleaning. Melvin used hay or straw for bedding. "Warm as toast," he said. "The worst thing you can do is to have too much heat in a kennel. I always kept windows and doors slightly open, even on cold nights. If I had shut the doors, I'd have had a hell of a mess to clean up in the morning, and with hounds free to come and go, they kept their fitness better."

Melvin kenneled his hounds and bitches together. "There're half as many fights when they're mixed," he said. He also always hunted a mixed pack.

A heat pen, pens for puppies and a cookhouse completed the kennel complex at Orange County in Melvin's years. "The heat pen was a good distance from the hound houses, and we had pens of various sizes for the pups," he said. "In my time, the cookhouse wasn't used for cooking because I fed flesh, but it had a meat grinder and a walk-in freezer to store flesh."

Melvin said the small kennel at Hume for the Bath County Hounds is a mini Orange County kennel. "It's all the same, in miniature, the porch, the beds, what have you, works great."

Feeding Hounds

When Melvin started as huntsman at Old Dominion, he emulated the hound feeding practices of his father. He boiled a big vat of water, threw in cornmeal or oatmeal, and sometimes added meat cooked the prior day. Basically, this was the same procedure used by Duke Leach at Orange County and most of the other huntsmen in the area at the time.

After a short time at Old Dominion, Melvin started to feed flesh. "I was convinced that raw meat was much better for dogs than cooked meat," he said. "When you cook meat, you cook out the [amino] acids. With flesh, right off, the dogs' coats bloom, and they have more stamina and energy. If you feed 'em right and give 'em good exercise, hounds will pick up in condition in a week, look like show hounds. Horses, of course, take much, much longer to come around."

Melvin said that hounds prefer cow meat. "It has more fat, is tenderer than horse meat," he said. "Also, it's important to feed the entire carcass—the heart, liver, rib cage, neck bones and legs, and blood is real good for dogs," he

In addition to the pictures on these pages, Mike Elmore's hound studies at the Orange County kennel are on pages 70/71 and 73.

A typical red ring-neck has a white chest and ring around the neck, and the tip of the tail is also white. "These dogs have a great tradition," Melvin said. "There's lots of packs that have gotten red ring-necks from us through the years in the United States and in England too, but we're the only pack that has a straight red pack."

Orange County Brian '76 is one of Melvin's all-time favorites. "He was champion at Virginia and Bryn Mawr, great in the field, and he sired champions. His name pops up in the pedigrees in hunts all over the country," Melvin said. Alexander Mackay-Smith was equally enthusiastic when describing Brian in *The Chronicle of the Horse*: "This is a remarkable hound, beautifully balanced with great substance and a very masculine head, long and full in the muzzle and wide between the eyes."

Brian's pedigree has strong line breeding, but there's also some out crossing, and in-breeding too. His sire, Nemo '68, was by Warrenton Finder '64, while in-breeding is evident in the appearance of Orange County Bagman '66 three generations back on the male side of Brian's pedigree, and twice on the female side four generations back.

Melvin said that when he bred within his own pack, the pups were nearly 100 percent true to Orange County's color standard. When out-crossed with Bull Run's red-and-white spotted hounds, he got about 50 percent.

Melvin estimated that in his years he bred at least 10 generations of Orange County hounds. "Breeding good-moving bitches to good-moving

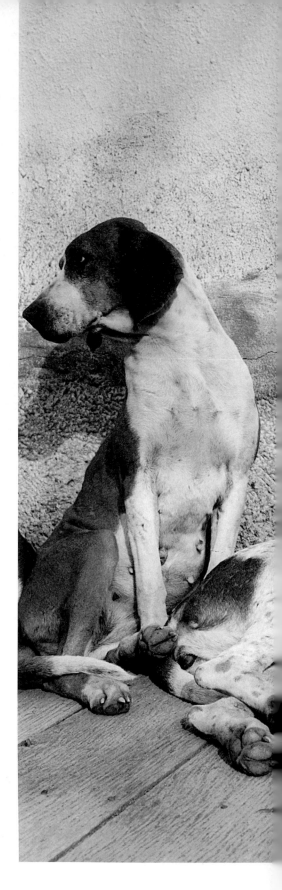

dogs really paid off," he said. "The way individual hounds move may be hard to notice when hounds are working in a pack, but like horses that move well, hounds will last a lot longer if they're good movers."

Melvin chuckled when recalling the mating of two tricolor hounds from Piedmont with an Orange County dog, when Albert was Piedmont's hunts-man. "We planned to divide the pups, me the reds, Albert the others," he said. "One bitch, though, lost her pups, and the other had 13, all red. One was real dark, and I gave him to Albert for a coon dog. I kept 12. Albert didn't send me any more bitches."

Melvin preferred to have his bitches whelp early. "The closer to the first of the year the better," he said. "Then if you show the pups, they're almost 18 months old, so they're more mature than pups that whelp late."

Melvin bred an average of 10 bitches a year at Orange County. "It's best for bitches to raise litters of six," he said. "When more than six, I'd usually cull to six. If a bitch had only three or four pups I'd usually keep them all. When culling, I'd first cull for color, then for size and character traits. If they're little as pups, they're going to be little later on, and you can pick the shy ones and the fighters out of litters. After culling, we'd end up with 35 to 40 puppies."

Training Puppies

At eight weeks, Melvin weaned the puppies at Orange County, and, right off, he turned them loose during daylight hours, given decent weather. "They don't learn a damned thing when they're penned up," Melvin said. "My way, they were free to wander around the yard, and leave the property for that matter. Their favorite spot was across the gravel county road, where they played in some high weeds and some water, and they scooted on the approach of cars. So much the better if they came across chickens, cows and calves. They had to get used to animals, and cars as far as that goes."

Peggy said that independence sometimes had a downside. "The puppies picked up brushes, curry combs and rub rags out of the barns, and any piece of clothing that was left out."

At an early age, Melvin got the puppies accustomed to his voice, which was soft when expressing approval and rough when disciplining. "If they fought, for instance, I'd yell something like, 'What the hell's going on, what's wrong with you.' They may not have listened, right off, but as they grew older, they paid attention. If not, I culled them real quick."

August 1, when the puppies were 17 or 18 months old, was an important date. By then, things at the kennel had slowed down, following Orange County's annual old-fashioned point-to-point, which Melvin frequently won, the hound shows and the haying season. The time had arrived to get down to serious work with the puppies. There wasn't time to waste, either, because the pups would start to be entered into the pack early that fall.

For the first two weeks, the puppies were coupled with entered hounds. "The whips and I, on horses, went with the pack around the yard and up and down the lane. The pups further got to know my voice and whistle," said Melvin.

While still coupled, Melvin took his hounds to Gordonsdale, a large farm across the road from the kennel, where lessons commenced for going to ground and casting. "There's lots of groundhog holes there. I'd use only fresh holes [ones currently in use], and when we got near, I sent the hounds. The entered hounds dragged the puppies to the hole, where I'd make a big fuss."

Melvin worked his pack at Gordonsdale to teach puppies to be responsive and maneuverable when being cast. "We'd often change direction, zigzagging across the large pastures, helped by my whips and my voice and

The kennel at the Poe's farm in Hume, Virginia, houses approximately 10 couple of Bath County's hounds. "In design, it's a mini Orange County kennel," said Melvin.

horn," Melvin said. He then started uncoupling hounds, the fast learners first, one or two at a time.

Some puppies, when uncoupled, burst ahead of the pack when going down farm lanes, out of range of being stung by Melvin's hunting whip. "For these, I kept a pocket full of small rocks," Melvin said. "I was an accurate thrower from my baseball years. When I hit the breakaways, they'd yelp, and the other pups took heed, too."

Melvin recalled one day when he was with a pack of puppies on the gravel road down from the kennel. "I was out of rocks and stopped to get off and fill my pockets," he said. "My horse, Danny, got away from me and took off up the road, followed by the pack. Danny turned down the kennel lane, where he was further riled by horses in a paddock. He ran round and round, the pups in tow, quite a sight."

By September 1, Melvin laid little drags around the kennel property to give the pups, uncoupled, the idea of hunting by scent. "The first day, the pups wouldn't run, waited by my side. Took two or three days for them to catch on," he said. Melvin then took six or eight puppies at a time to hunt live on Pignut Mountain, in the Bull Run range in back of the kennel.

Meanwhile, Melvin's method for training a deer-proof pack was under way. "I liked to expose puppies to deer. The more they'd see, the less the deer were a curiosity, the less they'd interest hounds," he said.

Pistols with bird shot, carried by the staff, were an integral part of deer-proofing. "I'd go out of my way to have each pup open on deer," Melvin said. "I cast them in a woods with wide wood rides, where I knew there were deer. I'd have whips on the wood rides, and when pups opened, they stung them good with bird shot. They remembered. Later, when tempted by deer, all's we had to do was fire the pistol in the air, and they associated the noise with pain. It's important that you shoot all your pups. If they go off and hunt deer on their own, they're deer hounds, and it's awfully hard to change 'em. You've got to nip this in the bud."

The cub hunting season at Orange County started in Melvin's time on September 15, with the members of the field present. "I'd put a few pups in the pack at first, then up it," Melvin said. "Cubbing is for training the young dogs, and also to train the cub foxes. I like to run a cub for a while, then pick up hounds, because you never want to den a young fox. If you let him run in a hole the first time you're after him, he'll keep running in holes. You want to make him think he's getting away. The more you do this, the better he's going to run."

Melvin often walks out the Bath County hounds to a nearby pond at the Poe farm at Hume on late summer afternoons.

CHAPTER 6

MELVIN'S WAY:
IN THE FIELD

SHORT SENTENCE pretty well sums up Melvin's practices in the field: Hunt the fox the natural way. To gain insight into his "natural way," I have divided this chapter into five sections: finding foxes, the use of voice and horn, the roles of whips and field master and his thoughts on scenting.

Finding Foxes

An oft-heard adage is that good huntsmen think like foxes, indeed are part fox. "Sure, you'd better think like foxes, understand them, or you're not going to make it as a huntsman," said Melvin. He explained that foxes, like all animals, are fond of sunshine, especially after cold winter nights. "If it's a sunny morning and the wind's blowing in from the north, foxes will be laying on the south side of hills, out of the wind. They'll lay in ground cover like multi-flora [rose], sedge grass or briers, especially along fence lines, where the sun can shine through the bushes," Melvin said. "If it's a moderate day, overcast and still, foxes will be most anywhere."

The Bath County pack drew a sedge field in the foothills of the Allegheny Mountains near Millboro Springs, Virginia, in 1993

When drawing wooded coverts, Melvin makes his hounds comb the woods. "The hounds must spread out," he said. "Especially with young hounds or when the scenting is bad, I often ride off the trails, right into the woods, to get my dogs to where the fox might be laying. If you stay on the path, the hounds will stay on the path with you, and that's not where foxes are."

After drawing a covert blank, Melvin doesn't waste time and effort waiting for hounds to exit the covert. "I want my dogs to hunt through a covert and right into the next one," he said. "Hopefully, the hounds were spread out in the blank covert, and move on to the next covert in the same way."

Melvin said if you wait for hounds to come out of a covert, you will be waiting on them the next time. "It's boring for foxhunters when a huntsman blows for 10 minutes or so to get all 40 hounds. Hell, you don't need 40 hounds to hunt a fox. I get rid of hounds that consistently linger in coverts."

Melvin pointed out that his no-wait philosophy doesn't pertain to hunting in Bath County. "There, we hunt only 16 or 18 dogs, and we got to get a fair portion of them out of coverts or we wouldn't have enough of a pack, so you'll hear me using my horn to call hounds out, and John [Coles] cracking his whip."

Melvin also has a no-wait policy when hounds put a fox to ground. "I don't get off my horse and make a big production of denning a fox. Oh sure, I'll blow my horn and tell my dogs that they've done good, but I won't let them linger at the den. I call these hounds den-diggers. I want to get on with things and find another fox. Persistent den-diggers are culled, because people don't come out hunting for a lot of standing around," Melvin said.

Voice and Horn

Melvin controls his hounds in the field by the tone of his voice. To encourage hounds when drawing, he uses a tender voice, sounding something like "hersh, hersh, hersh." I asked him what hersh means, was it "Humese" for hark? "I don't know," he said. "It doesn't make a damned bit of difference what you're saying, just so you're communicating with hounds, and I sometimes whistle softly when trying to sneak up on a fox."

When hounds speak on scent, Melvin uses a high-pitched voice, something like "hic, hic, hic" in rapid succession. When the line heats up, he uses increasingly higher pitch, a rebel yell-like scream, not unlike Peggy's "gone away" scream. These screams remind me somewhat of the loud barks of a fox on a quiet night.

Peggy Poe puts the finishing touches on Melvin's stock.

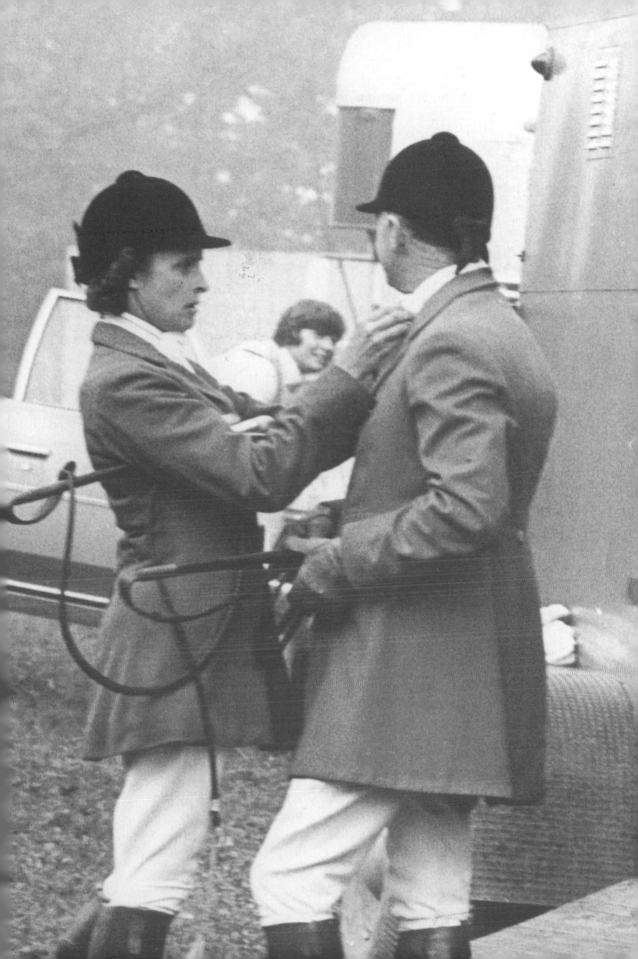

Orange County's pack of red ring-neck hounds negotiated a log panel at Kinross Farm in 1989.

Margaret White, hunting for the first time in Bath County after hunting behind Melvin for years at Orange County, remarked: "There's no voice like his, makes me shudder. That voice brings back all sorts of memories. When hounds hit a line, Melvin gave out with a scalded catlike yell that stirred hounds and followers, and even my old hunter sensed that something exciting was about to happen."

Melvin uses his voice throughout the day, sometimes four hours nonstop. He said your voice must come from your diaphragm, the wall of muscles and tendons between the cavity of the chest and the cavity of the abdomen. "If you rely on your mouth, it never works, you'll wear out your mouth," he said.

Melvin unbuttoned his shirt and pointed to a growth beneath his collarbone. "It popped up after a long day of hunting," he said. "The doctor said it's a calcium deposit. Reminds me of a splint on a horse's leg. It won't go away, but never bothers me, just an occupational hazard I guess of being a huntsman who uses his voice a lot."

"Nothing moves smooth as a fox except maybe a Cadillac," Melvin Poe said. He added that the faster a fox runs, the more scent he lays. "When the fox walks, the hounds walk."

Melvin never makes more noise than necessary when drawing coverts. "When hounds are fanned out in a covert, my voice is just loud enough that it carries to the outside hound," he said. "If you make too much noise, the fox is going to get up way ahead of you, so it'll take minutes before you get on him. You mustn't get the fox up until you're right on him, especially in dry weather and bad scenting, when it's hard to run a fox if he's got a start. Being close to the fox is the trick of the game."

Melvin said that every pack has a strike hound. "There's always one dog who'll strike at least 50 percent of the foxes," he said. "The strike hound isn't necessarily in front when combing a covert, but he knows where to go." Melvin screeches when the strike hound opens. "When I holler like that, the other dogs will stop and listen. They'll honor a good strike dog every time."

Melvin said that Orange County Barney '72 was the best strike hound he ever had. "We were having a slow day, just a couple short bursts," he said. "Suddenly, crossing General Heard's, Barney left the other hounds on the edge of a woods, hopped over a stone wall and went out in a pasture about

Bath County's American foxhounds worked a line out of the Bacova Briers in 2001.

150 yards to a rock pile. He put his nose up and scented the air. Then he lowered his head and sounded off. He jumped that fox hot. The other hounds joined Barney, and we had the damndest race you ever seen."

Melvin never blows "gone away" when hounds jump a fox. "You should never blow the horn to send hounds, just to call them," he said. "I stick that horn away and don't take it out until the fox is accounted for. I've seen huntsmen hooting and hollering and blowing their horn when hounds are on a line, and they're doing nothing but messing things up. Keep quiet, let the hounds work, that's my way. When hounds are running, people don't come out to listen to me, they come out to hear and follow the hounds."

However, Melvin does toot his horn a couple times at meets to signify it's time to move off. By then, the hounds have been present for 10 or 15 minutes. "I let them off the truck right away," said Melvin. "They're free to wander around, doing their thing," he said. "Some hounds socialize with the hunters. Some have favorite hounds. Other hounds wander around, some peeing on trailers, and some, mostly veterans, laying down and waiting. When I toot that horn, though, they know it's time to go to work."

Morton W. (Cappy) Smith led the first flight in a run with Orange County in 1974. Joan Smith is to Cappy's right, followed by Bruce Sundlun.

The Whips

For Melvin, the primary responsibilities for whips are to view foxes away and watch for deer. "Good whips are important, don't get me wrong, but my hounds were broke properly back in the kennel and the yard, and this makes it a lot simpler in the field because we've done our homework," he said.

John Coles recalled a day at Orange County when neither he nor Peggy could whip. "No big deal," said Melvin. "I'll be fine without you." I remember quite a few days in Bath County when Melvin was whipless.

Melvin said that it's very important that whips wait until the fox is out of sight before hollering to view him away. "Otherwise, the fox will run faster for the first distance," Melvin said. "Let him go off at his own pace, then he won't be as far in front of hounds."

The pistols carried by Melvin's whips are mostly shot in the air when wayward hounds open on deer. "I hated pistols and was a terrible shot,

Albert and Melvin Poe (right) forded the Jackson River with the Bath County pack in 2001. The Jackson, which runs through George Ohrstrom's Fassifern Farm, has some of the best trout fishing in Virginia.

but the sound itself was effective, carrying back to their early training," Peggy said.

Peggy dearly loved the hound Crosby, who was whelped in 1978. She handled Crosby to be a champion at the Virginia and Bryn Mawr shows. "One day Crosby left the pack and boo-hooed alone up though the woods, and I knew he was on deer," Peggy said. "He was a very sensitive hound, and I knew it would blow his mind to be shot. I cried, but there was nothing else I could do. I knew that this would be the last time he'd ever open on deer. There was no proof, though, because Crosby was hit and killed on the road shortly after."

Melvin doesn't approve of the use of two-way radios by whips. "I guess they're all right if you've got a lot of busy highways, like some hunts. However, I don't like any part of whips using radios to put hounds on a fox. There's no sport in that. Hell, let the whips view foxes away, just like it's been done for generations. Who needs radios? We don't need what some call the new way of foxhunting."

The Field Master

Melvin very much likes the field master to keep the field in close contact with him. "I want the followers right behind me, know where they're at," he said. "This way, they get a much better chance to see what's going on. To view a fox in my mind equals a two-mile gallop."

Melvin said that his way sometimes causes the followers to overrun hounds. "No big deal," he said. "All they got to do is stand still and be quiet, and the hounds more than likely will move straight through their horses' legs and be gone. In all probability there's no harm, and, if so, this is just a small downside of being up close, enjoying the hunt. Followers deserve this."

At Bath County, as field master I make every effort to stay right on Melvin's tail, especially since the territory is trappy, and sound doesn't travel well through gorges, dips and doodles and thick woods. During Hunt Week in 2000, when seven hunts in central Virginia grouped together to host a week of sport, we had 76 followers on our day. It was very misty when we moved off, and I got out of contact with Melvin right off the bat because he was being very quiet, trying to sneak up on a fox. For 10 or 15 minutes I stationed my field on top of a hill shrouded in mist, without the vaguest idea of where hounds were. Fortunately, John Coles galloped up. "Peter, he's way over on the Beach farm." We took off at a gallop and jumped two or three coops to get in contact with Melvin. Hounds, meanwhile, hadn't done a blessed thing, and, for that matter, we had a blank day. A member of the field rode at my side when hacking home. "Thanks, we saw some beautiful country once the fog lifted, and that was a hell of a run, the one early in the day." I didn't let on.

Scent

March is Melvin's favorite month. "I had more good hunts in March than any other month," he said. "Sure, this is partly because foxes are travelling for the breeding season, but the important reason is that scenting in March is great because the air is usually colder than the ground, and scent lays well."

November, on the other hand, is the worst month for Melvin because the air is usually warmer than the ground, and scent rises. "The air hasn't gotten cold yet," he said. "Also, dry spells in the fall make fallen leaves dry up. No moisture, no scent. All of this is bad for us huntsmen trying to show sport on opening meets and during what many think should be the height of the season."

Melvin said that September and October are usually good, that scenting gets better in December, and that January and February are dicey, depending on decent weather and footing. "If only they'd all be like March," he said.

Melvin said that changes in weather affect scent. "When fronts come through, scenting won't be as good as before or after the fronts," he said. "Sudden changes in temperature adversely affect scenting. The south wind is bad. Cool, damp days are best, especially when snow is in the air."

Melvin said that Capt. Ronnie Wallace of England explained his way of predicting scent at a seminar at the Virginia Hound Show. "He said if a car passes you on the road to the first covert and the hounds choke up on fumes, sneezing and coughing, you'll have a good scenting day. There's lots of truth in this," Melvin said. "At Bath County, I drive my truck from the kennel to the barn, about half mile away, and toot my hunting horn so the hounds follow along. When hounds choke or sneeze, I almost always have a decent day."

Melvin explained that the faster a fox runs, the more scent he lays. "When the fox walks, the hounds walk," he said. "When you get a fox up, he'll usually run to a certain spot and turn around and listen. If he doesn't hear hounds, the first thing you know he's walking. He won't run any more than he has to."

Melvin said that when a fox is at full speed, you can't see anything but a straight line, not like a horse or dog, where you can see strides. "Nothing runs as smooth as a fox, except maybe a Cadillac," he said.

Melvin told a story that proves that foxes give off practically no scent when they are still. "Orange County had a joint meet with Warrenton when Dick Bywaters was hunting Warrenton's pack," he said. "In a woods, I rode within 10 yards of a fox laying up on a stump. Four dogs went between me and the stump, one within 3 feet of the fox. Not a whisper. I could see the fox's eyes move as I went by."

Melvin caught up with Dick and told him about the fox on the stump. "Dick thought I said, 'My dogs killed a skunk.' When he finally understood what I was saying, he carried his dogs back to the stump, but the fox had gone. His dogs couldn't smell right off where he'd gone. The fox must have walked. Finally, Dick went down a hill, and hounds picked up a line and worked it slowly for a half an hour. The wind died down and the hounds adjusted. Damned if we didn't have a great day on my stump fox."

The Orange County Hunt hosts an old-fashioned point-to-point at the end of the hunting season each year in early April. Melvin Poe (# 12) won his share of these races in the 1970s.

CHAPTER 7

MELVIN'S WAY:
AT HOUND SHOWS

T HE LATE Charlie Whitehouse, M.F.H., complimented Melvin upon winning the first class of the day at the Bryn Mawr Hound Show in the late 1980s. Melvin responded: "Hell, you've got to win the first class if you're gonna win them all." The Orange County hounds did just that, sweeping every class in the American foxhound division.

Though a clean sweep was exceptional, consistent success was the rule during Melvin's tenure, when Orange County won 18 of 24 renewals of the coveted five-couple pack class at Bryn Mawr and 19 of 24 at the Virginia Hound Show. These awesome statistics are engraved on a silver tray presented to Melvin at his retirement party in 1991.

Melvin said there's no secret to this success. "First, you've got to breed hounds that move good, and if they move right they'll have good conformation. Then, you've got to train 'em so they'll show themselves off, and it doesn't hurt to have showmanship by the handlers, and to use some tricks that have worked for me through the years."

Melvin credits Chrissy with raising the puppies correctly. "She was president of the puppies," he said. "She did all the puppy work, right from whelping, through weaning and fitting them for showing. She played with

Peggy Poe's particular favorite was Orange County Crosby '79, who was the champion American foxhound at the Bryn Mawr Hound Show in 1981.

'em, fed 'em, and as they grew she'd pit one against the other to pick out the best. As show time approached, she'd have a good handle on which of the 25-some puppies in the kennel were the best."

Peggy said that early on and through the hunting season, Melvin didn't pay much attention to Chrissy's claims of outstanding puppies. "However, when hunting was over in early April, he became very attentive," she said.

Hunt members enjoyed coming to the kennel to help prepare and show entries in Orange County's puppy show, annually held on the first Sunday in May, the weekend of the Virginia Gold Cup. They walked puppies on the leash and groomed and lavished attention on them on boards, similar to the boards on which hounds are judged at shows. "The secret was spending real time for a tremendous amount of walking, grooming, handling and standing them properly," said Mike du Pont.

The puppy shows were held at various farms in the hunting territory. "To get away was good for the pups, got 'em used to what was ahead," said Melvin. "For showing a class winner, grown-ups got a bottle of my wine and children $5. It was always a fun day, something everyone looked forward to."

*Melvin Poe worked hard to win the five-couple pack class for Orange County
at the Virginia Foxhound Show in 1975.*

During Melvin Poe's near 30-year career, the Orange County Hunt won 18 of 24 renewals of the coveted five-couple pack class at the Bryn Mawr Hound Show and 19 of 24 at the Virginia Foxhound Show. In 1984, Orange County's masters, James L. Young (left) and W. H. (Mike) du Pont (center), joined Melvin in the trophy presentation at the Virginia show.

The staff showed hounds at the Virginia show on the Sunday of Memorial Day weekend and at Bryn Mawr the following Friday. "We'd divide up the hounds," said Chrissy. "Melvin had the ones he was particularly fond of, and Mom, Butch and I got the rest, and I remember that Mr. du Pont occasionally showed a hound or two when he was master."

Working with hounds to attain fitness and obedience for the pack class was the responsibility of the staff, and principally Melvin. "We'd pick 15 dog hounds and narrow it down to the best 10 for show day," Melvin said. "We never used bitches because we had to have a level pack in size as well as color, and we didn't use unentered hounds. The shows were a month after we stopped hunting, so I kept my pack hounds fit by driving my truck around the fields at the kennel and at Gordonsdale, tooting my [hunting] horn all the while, the hounds following. Fitness was important because some of the hounds in the pack class showed in other classes during the day, and they'd get tired if unfit, particularly in hot weather."

For obedience, Melvin and the whips worked with the pack on foot. "I'd be in front and hold up my hands and teach 'em to stop and stand, and when they moved off they'd have to pack up good. It took time, but we'd end up with a pack that was fit and obedient."

The hounds were bathed on the day before the show. "You'd have to be careful," said Melvin. "If you got soap up their butts, their tails often wouldn't go up on show day, and that was very bad."

Melvin's tricks came into play at the show. "I always was first to enter the ring, and I'd move off fast," Melvin said. "Of course I had to have a good moving hound, but the judges would see my hound first, and they'd use him, if impressed, as a standard for judging the others."

Peggy and Chrissy said that Melvin had particular success with dog hounds. "He used some tricks, too, in getting his hounds attentive, making them gay, bursting with energy," Peggy said. "His quiet little whistle was effective, but there was more than that. For a timid hound, the nasty old man would have the scent of an in heat bitch on a tissue and wave it at the nose of his hound at the in-gate. That hound would really come to life, enter the ring on his toes."

Chopped-up liver, fried chicken and Melvin's wine had important roles at hound shows. "We'd give hounds a good whiff of the liver, then put it in plastic bags in the pockets of our white show coats," Peggy said. "That got their attention, but during the day the bags sometimes leaked and we had brown stains."

Melvin has long had a weakness for fried chicken. He's never been able to get past a Hardee's at the halfway point of the drive to Bath County, and he always bought a couple barrels on the way to hound shows. "We'd do some serious chicken eating at the lunch break, and I'd round up the bones and feed 'em to my dogs just before the pack class," Melvin said. I'd keep the smell of chicken on my hands. The hounds' eyes, their heads, followed my hands in the class."

When show champions were in the pack, Melvin would call out their names within earshot of the judges. "I'd call out, 'Look here, Brian, look here,' because the presence of dogs that they'd pinned earlier in the day seemed to impress judges," Melvin said.

Orange County Busty '80 was one of Chrissy Gray's favorite hounds. In 1982, Busty was the champion American foxhound at the Virginia Foxhound Show.

Veteran hound show judge Sherman Haight explained his ideas of why Melvin had such success in pack classes: "Of course he had fine hounds and a nice level pack, but there was far more to it. He was very quiet with his hounds. He was always smiling, and the tone of his voice was proper, and that's terribly important. Hounds may not understand the words you're using, but they certainly do understand the tone of your voice. If you're tense, they're tense. If you're smiling, they're smiling. Melvin's hounds were always very relaxed, and that's terribly impressive to anyone who's judging a pack class. Some hounds may do exactly what they're supposed to do, but they're not looking happy. Their sterns may be up, but they're sort of wooden in the way they do things. Not the case with Melvin's hounds. They were obviously having a good time, and Melvin had that thread with his hounds that you have to earn as a huntsman."

Vicky Crawford of the Potomac Hunt echoed Haight's feelings: "Melvin made things effortless when showing hounds. Others worked so hard; he was so casual. He knew he was good; he knew his hounds were good. His hounds were part of him."

Chrissy said she got nervous in whipping-in to Melvin in the pack class. "It was the one class we'd won so often, the one we had to win. Potomac was always tough, but we had a little secret weapon. We'd give Larry [Larry Pitts, Potomac's longtime huntsman] a glass of Melvin's wine at the lunch break."

Peggy said that Bryn Mawr was their favorite show. "In our day, it was *the* show. Now, Virginia rivals it, maybe surpasses it, but we really loved Bryn Mawr. It was like a vacation, the chance to get away for a couple days and be with old friends."

Success at Bryn Mawr in the early 1970s paved the way for what became known as Orange County's Landowners' Party. "We'd done real well that year, but hardly any members were there," said Melvin. "Mrs. Furness [wife of the master and a big supporter of the Poes] called to congratulate us. I said, 'Well, let's get the members over to our place, we'll roast a pig and show off the winners and trophies.' Champion hounds posed on the front porch and the pack class winners strutted their stuff."

The Landowners' Party in early July became an annual fixture. "It was great," said Mike du Pont. "Not all the guests were 'swells.' They were there, but also the local farmers from down the road and farm managers, too. If we had a big, swish cocktail party, perhaps the farmers and farm managers wouldn't have felt comfortable. At Melvin and Peggy's, everyone had a good time."

CHAPTER 8

THANKS, MELVIN

 EEDLESS TO SAY, Melvin has touched the lives of countless. When word got around that a book on Melvin was in the works, many of his admirers made comments about their favorite huntsman.

MORTON W. (CAPPY) SMITH (MASTER OF ORANGE COUNTY 1971-1979)

Cappy Smith is known as a perfectionist, one who wants things done right. "At Orange County I wasn't concerned about everything being perfect. I had the best huntsman in the United States, and I let him alone," Cappy said. "Melvin was as fine a person as a huntsman—warm, personable, genuine. Everyone connected with Orange County—everywhere, for that matter—thought the world of him. He related as well to people as to his hounds and horses."

WILLIAM H. (MIKE) DU PONT (MASTER OF ORANGE COUNTY 1979-1987)

Mike du Pont commenced hunting with Orange County in 1962, the same year that Melvin came to the hunt. About 15 years later, Cappy Smith asked Mike to take the field for a day. "I was terrified, leading the field with

W. H. (Mike) du Pont, who was the master of the Orange County Hunt in 1979-1987, enjoyed hunting with the Bath County Hounds in 2001.

the great Melvin Poe in front of me," Mike said. "I'd read all those rules about giving plenty of room to the huntsman and hounds, not interfering, never getting on the line, never turning the fox. Early on that day, Melvin signaled me to come forward and said, 'Stay close, let 'em see what foxhunting is all about. There's nothing you can do to mess things up.'"

When Mike became master and took the field on a regular basis, he and Melvin developed what Mike described as telepathic rapport. "I could tell by the way he turned his head or shook his crop where he wanted the field. He sometimes placed us on a hill overlooking the covert being drawn, with the hope that we could view the fox," Mike said.

Mike said that Melvin was always very secure in himself, every step of what he was doing. "He instilled that in others," Mike said. "The greatest thing about Melvin, though, was his real love of his job, the joy of being out there doing something he really loved. He was happy, content with himself. That demeanor, that spirit, was contagious. It filtered to the staff, the masters, to the front of the field, to the back of the field, and I'm certain to his hounds. Everyone was having a good time because Melvin was having a good time."

JAMES L. YOUNG (MASTER OF ORANGE COUNTY 1982-PRESENT; FORMER PRESIDENT OF THE MASTERS OF FOXHOUNDS ASSOCIATION; SON OF ROBERT B. YOUNG, MASTER OF ORANGE COUNTY 1947-1952)

Jimmy Young has had many good times in hunting with Melvin, but one incident sticks out in his mind on a day when foxes, hounds, field and staff seemed to have particular fun.

"We had many short races on foxes over two of our traditional fixtures, Turner Mountain and Kinloch Farm. After five hours of good hunting, the field had dwindled to about six and staff. As we were drawing the hounds back to the meet, they struck on a fox at the base of a small, wooded mountain with a stream defining its lower boundary to the right of the sloping horse fields through which we were traversing. As we stood on the side of a hill, listening and occasionally glimpsing hounds running in the wooded covert along the base of the hillock beneath us, one member whispered, 'Is that a fox above us?' 'No,' said Melvin. 'It's two foxes.' Indeed, as we looked up the hill, there were two foxes sitting outside a nest of dens, watching the hunt unfold just as we were. Gently, we all edged up the side of the field until we were standing together within 20 yards of the foxes and their dens.

"As the hounds passed us below and to the left, with their chorus reverberating off the shadowed foothills, we caught a glimpse of the hunted fox as he made a turn uphill around us. Our vulpine compatriots shifted their seats

James L. Young, the former president of the Masters of Foxhounds Association, has been a master of the Orange County Hunt since 1982.

and their gazes to follow their comrade as he slowly made a great circle route up the hill and then straight back towards their den.

"The final act unfolded within yards of the sparse audience. First one, then the other foxy spectator slipped into the den as the hounds moved closer. Then the hunted quarry breasted the rise, trotted to the earth, and stood staring at us, almost in greeting. With unhurried grace he watched the approaching pack and then with typically venatic aplomb he slid into the lair. It was a sublime moment, and it taught us all that it pays to stay to the end."

JOHN COLES (MASTER OF ORANGE COUNTY 2001 TO PRESENT; FREQUENTLY A WHIPPER-IN AND OCCASIONALLY THE SUBSTITUTE HUNTSMAN AT ORANGE COUNTY AND BATH COUNTY FROM 1977 TO THE PRESENT)

John recalls a day's hunting in 1977 that brought home Melvin's instincts as a woodsman and his eagle-like eyesight. "It was opening meet, at Whitewood, the first year I hunted with Melvin," John said. "The wind was blowing hard when hounds jumped a fox in the first piece of woods we drew. Right off, they got away from us. Melvin started galloping, with Peggy and me, as whips, right behind, followed by a field of 75 or so. We never heard a hound, not a peep. I said to myself, 'What in the world is this man doing, just giving us a good gallop?'

"We galloped for more than an hour, to the north and west in a big circle, and ended up down near Marshall, where, suddenly, we saw hounds at an earth, where they'd put their fox to ground after what must have been a seven-mile point. Only a handful of followers were still with us."

John asked Melvin how he knew where hounds had gone. "Simple," Melvin said. "In the woods, I studied the leaves, could see where they'd been turned over, where hounds had been. In open fields, I could see where hounds had pushed the broom sedge down. I had to do some zigzagging, but there were signs all along of my hounds."

This hunt gave John a good chance to see Melvin's style of riding. "He'd be galloping along under a loose rein, paying no attention to his horse, preoccupied with other things. He'd pull down to a trot two or so strides from fences. Then he'd snatch his horse a couple times to get his attention, kick him and pop over. In all the years I've hunted with Melvin, he's hasn't varied from this style, and never, knock wood, have I seen him have a fall over a fence."

John said that Melvin gets along with horses, just like his rapport with hounds. "They like him," John said. "Many of the horses given to the hunt were ex-racehorses. In his last couple years with Orange County, when he was near 70, Melvin hunted Anne's Lover, a real rank steeplechase horse who used to run off with jockeys. Melvin and Anne's Lover got along great, perfectly relaxed."

GENE HACKLEY (EMPLOYEE OF THE ORANGE COUNTY HUNT 1968 TO PRESENT)

The friendship of the Poe and Hackley families goes back several generations. Both families were originally from Amissville in Rappahannock County. To this day, Poes Road runs through Hackleys Crossroad in that area, but, like the Poes, the Hackleys moved in time to the Hume area in Fauquier County. "My daddy used to sell moonshine to Mr. Ollie Poe [Melvin's father]," Gene said. "Hell, Melvin's known me since before I knew myself."

Gene's duties at the kennels have included cutting trails, and, according to Gene, "just about anything that needs to be done." Melvin and Gene also often get together for deer and turkey hunting, and they kept and trained bird dogs for quail shooting.

The friendship of Gene and Melvin, then, goes, far deeper than the typical boss-employee relationship. "We're like brothers," Gene said. Melvin agreed.

Gene Hackley (right) has worked at the Orange County kennel since 1968. In their spare time, Gene and Melvin go bird and deer hunting together. "We're like brothers," Gene said.

CHARLES T. MATHESON (FOXHUNTER, LANDOWNER AND PRESIDENT OF THE ORANGE COUNTY HUNT)

Charley and his wife Bonnie got their starts in hunting with Orange County through the Poes. "When Bonnie bought her own hunter in 1965, she boarded him at Peggy and Melvin's," Charley said. "At the time, we were living in Washington and came to a country cottage on weekends. The Poes were so nice to us, so encouraging. It was always fun to go there."

Peggy was shelved with a broken ankle at one point during Bonnie's early days at Orange County. "Peggy and I followed hunts in a truck," Charley said. "I'd hunted a bit as a youngster with my father at Casanova. Driving around with Peggy reminded me of the fun I was missing. I took up hunting again in 1970 and kept my horse, along with Bonnie's, at the Poes."

Charley became a member of the hunt's board of stewards, and he was the president for five years, succeeding George Ohrstrom. "Melvin of course showed great sport through the years, but there's so much more to him," Charley said. "Everybody likes to be around him. He's an old-fashioned character, a folk hero of sorts. People are drawn to him, love to get his insight into things they're very much interested in. Melvin has the knack of simplifying things that could be complicated."

Charley said that Melvin never got down on things when hunting, accepted the good with the bad. "In the hunting field, I never saw him be untoward to anybody, including some people in charge who kind of deserved it at times. He was always great with people and, of course, with his hounds. He was the ultimate professional."

Charley said that during his tenure as president, Orange County, like most hunts, invariably ran at a deficit, always needed more money than was taken in through subscriptions and fund raisers. "This caused some to suggest that we should save by using honorary staff members. Not the way I look at it. Orange County has always gone with professionals, and I hope we always stay a professional hunt."

SHERMAN P. HAIGHT (MASTER AND HUNTSMAN OF THE LITCHFIELD COUNTY HOUNDS IN CONNECTICUT, FREQUENT JUDGE AT MAJOR HOUND SHOWS)

Sherman Haight attempted to explain Melvin's success with show hounds. "Very few have the understanding of the time it takes to prepare hounds to show properly. You can breed hounds that have all the greatest physical attributes, in all the right proportions, but it all goes to waste if you don't spend an immense amount of time to develop what I call 'presence.' With presence, hounds can go into the ring and feel, 'We're not imbued by anything, we're going to take all this in stride.' Developing this presence in hounds is the product of a tremendous amount of hard work. It's more than work, though. Some huntsmen are very good at it, and their hounds come in and they stand exactly the way they're supposed to stand, but they're sort of wooden because they know damned well they better, or else. You never saw that with Melvin. They were trying to please him. They knew what he wanted and they gave it to him because they wanted to please him, not because 'by God we better do it or somebody's going to lay a hand on us.' They were looking at him. What do you want us to do next? That's the relationship that Melvin Poe had with his hounds."

DR. HUGH B. LYNN (FOXHUNTER AND LANDOWNER WITH ORANGE COUNTY)

Dr. Lynn remembers Melvin for being a close friend of his family and for his showmanship and rapport with people of all backgrounds. He cited an example of Melvin's love of showing people a good time, and the more present the better.

"Melvin knew that I was often called upon at the Mayo Clinic to give lectures," Dr. Lynn said. "I phoned Melvin on the evening of a day when I couldn't hunt, and asked him how things went. 'It was all right, but only eight or so were in the field,' he said. He asked me how I'd feel if I worked hard to prepare for a lecture and only eight people showed up."

As to Melvin's rapport with people in every station of life, Dr. Lynn recalled that upon arriving early at a meet he saw Melvin and Jackie Onassis on their hands and knees. "I wondered what in the world was going on," said Dr. Lynn. "I discovered that Melvin was pointing out to his friend the tracks of a beaver."

KERRY GLASS (MASTER AND HUNTSMAN OF THE NORFOLK HUNT, MASSACHUSETTS)

Kerry was philosophic in describing the essence of her old friend Melvin Poe, and she fears his beliefs and practices are being threatened in the urbanization of much of rural America.

"Melvin is far more than a huntsman," Kerry said. "He's a man of the land. He has lived in a world of farming, forest and fishing. He is in tune with the land and all that grows and lives on it. He understands the habits and behavior of all wildlife and the impact and effect of each season. It was necessary for him to understand all that nature offers, for as a youth his family's livelihood depended on it. He has passed that knowledge on as a Boy Scout leader and later as a huntsman. He has shown many the beauty of the countryside; he has instructed many in wildlife tracking and behavior.

"Sad to say, though, the countryside and many aspects of the rural habitat that Melvin knows and loves are becoming threatened. His concepts of farming, crops, cover and rural character are slowly being replaced by the views of a new breed of landowners in Virginia and other areas. Do the new owners understand the needs of wildlife and how crucial are crops, cover, forest and wetlands to the balance of nature? Do they sense the need of shelter and food for fish, fur and feathered friends in the rural region?

"If only Melvin Poe—the farmer, huntsman and fisherman—could pass on his wisdom to the new breed of country dwellers, the countryside and its creatures could flourish," Kerry concluded.

NORMAN FINE (FOXHUNTER WITH THE BLUE RIDGE HUNT AND EDITOR OF *COVERTSIDE*, THE OFFICIAL PUBLICATION OF THE MASTERS OF FOXHOUNDS ASSOCIATION)

"Yes, I remember the great runs that Joan and I always enjoyed when visiting the Orange County Hunt, but what stands out most in our minds— and we speak of it often—is how Melvin's hounds adored him. Many huntsmen hustle their hounds onto the hound truck after a hunt, the theory being, capture them while they're still here. Not so, Melvin. After hunts, he just let them hang out. They weren't about to leave; they were where they wanted to be. With him. The door of the hound truck always remained open while Melvin offered his homemade wine to the foxhunters. Some hounds would climb in, others would lie on the ramp at his feet outside. They were relaxed and happy, and, if they weren't snoozing, their eyes followed his every move in complete adoration. This is something you can't train hounds to do."

MARGARET R. WHITE (FOXHUNTER, LANDOWNER AND MEMBER OF THE BOARD OF STEWARDS OF ORANGE COUNTY)

"It was absolutely special, those 28 years I had hunting with Melvin at Orange County," Margaret said. "There was a lot more to it, though, than just that. I have great fondness for Peggy and Melvin. We had children together in Pony Club [Margaret was the D.C. with Eve Fout of the Middleburg Orange County Pony Club]. What fun our families had together, and very good riders came out of M.O.C. in those years, like the Poe children, Gould and Skip Brittle, Denny Brown, Tommy Skiffington, Al Quanbeck and Nina, Dougie and Virginia Fout. These kids went on to fun and success in various ways with horses—foxhunting, eventing, steeplechasing and showing. It all started with riding across country behind the Pony Club's beagle pack, then with Melvin at Orange County."

Margaret R. White enjoyed hunting with Melvin Poe at Orange County for 28 years. She is a major landowner in the Orange County territory and a member of the hunt's board of stewards.

EVE FOUT (FOXHUNTER, LANDOWNER AND MEMBER OF THE BOARD OF STEWARDS OF ORANGE COUNTY)

Eve is the sole person I've met who occasionally hunted with Melvin at Old Dominion—her parents were close friends of Col. and Mrs. Hinckley—then regularly each year during Melvin's long tenure at Orange County. "It seemed like we were part of Melvin's family when we were out there [hunting]," she said. "I particularly remember him for his way with children. He was as nice to young kids, my own included, as to very important older people like Jackie Kennedy [a lifelong friend who kept her hunters at the Fout's farm]. He took the kids to the kennel to show them 'his dogs' as he called hounds, took them coon hunting at night, and he was the 'chief honcho' for the overnight ride and games put on each summer for Pony Clubbers by Nick Arundel. Kids never forget things like this."

Eve said that Peggy, despite being tied down with duties at the hunt and with the bed and breakfast and boarding stable at Hume, always provided a marvelous home for Melvin, her children and many others who looked at being at the Poes as a second home. "She made it a great place to raise kids. She's quite a lady," said Eve.

Marshall Hawkins
photographed Jacqueline
Kennedy Onassis and
Morton W. Smith, MFH,
at a meet at George L.
Ohrstrom's Whitewood
Farm in 1979.

Letters

Melvin received letters from fellow foxhunters from far and wide upon his retirement in 1991:

BENJAMIN H. HARDAWAY III (MASTER AND HUNTSMAN OF THE MIDLAND FOX HOUNDS IN GEORGIA AND FORMER PRESIDENT OF THE MASTERS OF FOXHOUNDS ASSOCIATION)

I consider Melvin Poe the premier huntsman in the United States. However, it's not only his ability with hounds that make him so impressive, but the fact that he is an exceptional human being… The main thing he had was his enthusiasm. Every day, he imparted this to the field and the hounds.

JACQUELINE KENNEDY ONASSIS (FOXHUNTER WITH ORANGE COUNTY)

Congratulations, dear Melvin, on your glorious career. No one who hunted with you will ever forget the wonderful days you gave us. With gratitude and all my happiest wishes for the future.

PRESIDENT RONALD REAGAN (FORMER FOXHUNTER WITH THE WEST HILLS HUNT IN CALIFORNIA)

I am delighted to join with your family and friends in offering my warm congratulations on your retirement from active hunt service. The loyalty and dedication you have brought to your more than thirty years of service with the Orange County Hunt have earned you the respect and affection of all who know and work with you. Indeed, you have deservedly earned the title, "The Dean of American huntsmen." May the years to come be as productive and rewarding. Nancy joins me in wishing you every happiness and God's richest blessing.

SENATOR JOHN W. WARNER (FOXHUNTER WITH ORANGE COUNTY)

Please accept my warm congratulations on the occasion of your retirement. I know that the commitment demonstrated by your many years of service will continue to serve as an inspiration to others for years to come . . . I value your friendship greatly

C. WILLIAM BERMINGHAM (MASTER OF THE HAMILTON HUNT IN CANADA AND FORMER PRESIDENT OF THE MASTERS OF FOXHOUNDS ASSOCIATION)

Congratulations on an outstanding career. You have set a record for good sport and great hounds that will stand for many years. The Orange County foxes will be celebrating tonight!

CAPTAIN R. E. WALLACE (MASTER OF THE EXMOOR IN ENGLAND AND CHAIRMAN OF ENGLAND'S MASTERS OF FOXHOUNDS ASSOCIATION)

Your achievement in showing good sport and in breeding and improving the American foxhound has obtained worldwide fame. I send you and your family warmest wishes on behalf of many that have enjoyed your company from this side of the Atlantic.

Two of America's most respected huntsmen – Benjamin H. Hardaway III (left) of the Midland Fox Hounds in Georgia and Melvin Poe – enjoyed hunting together in Virginia in 1988.

BRUCE SUNDLUN (FOXHUNTER WITH ORANGE COUNTY AND GOVERNOR OF RHODE ISLAND)

Thank you for our years of foxhunting, which has changed the lives of Marjorie and me. Thank you for courtesy when we did not do well, and thank you for the encouragement when we did. You must feel a security that few people can, because you are very good at what you do, and you help others less able to enjoy what you do well.

WILLIAM N. WILBUR (FORMER MASTER OF THE WARRENTON HUNT)

I know that retiring from what you have done for so long and so well is a big jolt. I can relate to how you feel because stopping hunting was a real turnaround in my life. I had sixty years of hunting, and I'm sure you had that much or more. Well, perhaps we are lucky to get through it without serious and long lasting injuries. I had only three broken collarbones! Anyway, you now have time to do things you probably couldn't fit in with all the responsibilities that your job laid on you.

C. MARTIN WOOD III (MASTER OF THE LIVE OAK HOUNDS IN FLORIDA AND FORMER PRESIDENT OF THE MASTERS OF FOXHOUNDS ASSOCIATION)

Your contribution to the wonderful sport of foxhunting has been so great that it is not measurable. No one can accurately assess how much your investment of time, expertise and single-minded dedication has meant to our sport, although tangible evidence exists everywhere: in the form of consistent success of your foxhounds at major hound shows; in the fact that bloodlines developed by your breeding programs can now be found in major kennels around the world; and, most important, in the exemplary sport you have shown with the Orange County hounds during your long tenure as their huntsman ... Melvin Poe is, in fact, a legend in his own time. Current sporting literature already chronicles your exploits. Future writing about the history of foxhunting will bear testimony to your brilliance as a huntsman for new generations of foxhunters to learn from. It is a record not easily surpassed and one in which you should take great pride.

MARY JAMIESON (FOXHUNTER WITH THE RAPPAHANNOCK HUNT IN VIRGINIA AND JOURNALIST)

This is a wine with a difference, a peach flavored, sparkling wine. [Mary described a bottle of wine given to Melvin at his retirement party.] It reminds me

of you, Melvin. It is not only good, but it has an added difference. It's the added difference that has made you a genius among those of your chosen profession, like a Babe Ruth, a Jack Dempsey, a Red Grange. Among huntsmen, there is Melvin Poe.

DR. FREDERICK F. WARREN (A KEY LANDOWNER IN ORANGE COUNTY'S TERRITORY)

We appreciate Mr. Poe's consideration of our crops and stock, and his pleasant personality made life enjoyable.

The best testimonial on Melvin has been saved for last. It's from his granddaughter, Melissa Paradise, age 10, who submitted an essay on her grandfather as a school assignment:

Melissa Paradise, 10, wrote a moving essay titled "Grandpa Melvin" as a school assignment.

Grandpa Melvin

My Grandpa's name is Melvin Poe. He is 80 years old. Despite his age, he is a very active man. He has lived on a farm in Virginia for all of his life and grew up riding horses. Every day he wakes up and works for 10 hours a day. My Grandpa has a great sense of humor and he always makes people laugh. He has lots of stories and jokes that he tells people and everyone loves to listen to him talk.

My Grandpa is a famous foxhunter. For more than 30 years he was the huntsman for the Orange County Hunt. People came from all over the world to hunt with him. There have been many books and newspaper stories written about my Grandpa. He even had a movie made about his life. Through foxhunting he has met some very famous people. Jackie Onassis was one of the people that used to hunt with him. They were good friends and she was a big fan of my Grandpa's. Today, my Grandpa has retired from the big hunt, but he has his own pack of hounds and he still hunts today.

My Grandpa has had an interesting life. He was one of ten children and grew up on a farm. He spent his spare time playing baseball and foxhunting. When he was 22, he was drafted into World War II. He spent two years in France as an Army mechanic. The war was so bad that he won't ever fly on planes again. Any time he comes to visit us in Minnesota he takes the train. I like to hear him talk about the war. He only tells funny stories instead of scary stuff.

My Grandpa and I are very close. I am his first grandchild. When I was younger, I remember going fishing for the first time ever with him. We had a blast. I also remember when I was younger he took my Mom and I foxhunting. It was my first time out with him and it was very special for me. I have very good memories of spending time with my Grandpa. One time I remember we went to pick raspberries on the farm. We picked them for hours and had a whole bucket full. When we came back, we just sat outside and ate every last one.

My Grandpa is very special to me because of many things. He is kind to people and is well respected. He is honest, good and liked by everyone. He has a great life and he appreciates everything around him. He understands nature, loves animals and is always happy. He loves his family and they all love him. I hope that I can be just like him.

So do a lot of people, Melissa.

Picture Credits

Dust jacket cover – McIntyre Photography

Dust jacket rear cover – Janet Hitchen

Dust jacket front flap – Douglas Lees

Pages 4-5 – Giny Hunter

Page 8 – Douglas Lees

Page 10 – Peter Winants

Pages 10-11 – Unknown, *The Chronicle of the Horse* collection

Page 12 – Unknown, National Sporting Library collection

Page 13 – Unknown, National Sporting Library collection

Pages 14-15 – Marshall P. Hawkins, National Sporting Library Collection

Page 16 – Unknown

Page 18 – Unknown

Page 19 – Unknown

Page 20 – Peter Winants

Page 21 – Peter Winants

Page 23 – Illustration by Elizabeth R. Manierre

Page 25 – Unknown

Page 26 – Unknown

Pages 28-29 – Douglas Lees

Pages 30-31 – Unknown

Page 32 – Marshall P. Hawkins, National Sporting Library collection

Pages 34-35 – Douglas Lees

Pages 36-37 – Douglas Lees

Pages 40-41 – Marshall P. Hawkins

Pages 46-47 – Unknown, courtesy of George L. Ohrstrom

Page 49 – Peter Winants

Page 50 – John Coles

Page 53 – Douglas Lees

Page 54 – Davenport Films

Page 57 – Unknown

Page 60 – Unknown

Page 61 – Peter Winants

Page 62 – Mike Elmore

Page 65 – Janet Hitchen

Page 66 – Janet Hitchen

Pages 68-69 – Mike Elmore

Pages 70-71 – Mike Elmore

Page 72-73 – Mike Elmore

Page 74 – Peter Winants

Page 77 – Janet Hitchen

Pages 78-79 – Woods Winants

Page 81 – Unknown

Page 82 – Douglas Lees

Page 83 – Marshall P. Hawkins, *The Chronicle of the Horse* collection

Page 84 – Douglas Lees

Page 85 – Marshall P. Hawkins, *The Chronicle of the Horse* collection

Pages 86-87 – John Coles

Pages 90-91 – Unknown

Page 92 – Freudy Photo, *The Chronicle of the Horse* collection

Pages 94-95 – Douglas Lees

Page 96 – Unknown

Page 98 – James D. Carr, *The Chronicle of the Horse* collection

Page 100 – Douglas Lees

Page 103 – Mary Coker

Page 104-105 – Peter Winants

Page 109 – Douglas Lees

Pages 110-111– Marshall P. Hawkins, National Sporting Library collection

Page 112 – Marshall P. Hawkins, *The Chronicle of the Horse* collection

Pages 114-115 – Unknown

Page 116 – Patti Gould

Index